Gesture, Gender, Nation

Gesture, Gender, Nation

Dance and Social Change in Uzbekistan

Mary Masayo Doi

Bergin & Garvey
Westport, Connecticut • London

Library of Congress Cataloging-in-Publication Data

Doi, Mary Masayo.
 Gesture, gender, nation : dance and social change in Uzbekistan / Mary Masayo Doi.
  p. cm.
 Includes bibliographical references and index.
 ISBN 0–89789–825–7 (alk. paper)
  1. Dance—Social aspects—Uzbekistan. 2. Women—Uzbekistan—Social conditions.
 3. Uzbekistan—Social conditions—20th century. I. Title.
 GV1700.7.D65 2002
 306.4'84—dc21   2001035115

British Library Cataloguing in Publication Data is available.

Library of Congress Catalog Card Number: 2001035115
ISBN: 0–89789–825–7

First published in 2002

Bergin & Garvey, 88 Post Road West, Westport, CT 06881
An imprint of Greenwood Publishing Group, Inc.
www.greenwood.com

Printed in the United States of America

The paper used in this book complies with the
Permanent Paper Standard issued by the National
Information Standards Organization (Z39.48–1984).

10 9 8 7 6 5 4 3 2 1

To my parents,
and
Anya Peterson Royce

Contents

Prologue

The expressive arts played a dramatic and highly visible role in the former Soviet empire. Unlike the United States, the arts in the Soviet Union received extensive public support through state-sponsored schools to train professional dancers and performing troupes such as the great Kirov and Bolshoi ballet companies. At the regional level, the famous pan–Soviet Moiseyev company toured the world featuring "national" dances representing the diverse republics and peoples comprising the Soviet Union. Why did the Soviet government choose dance as a political medium? How did the expressive arts affect Soviet society, and how did such close links with the state affect art and artists? What did it mean to be an artist trained and employed by a colonial government?

When the Soviet Union collapsed in 1991, firsthand field research became a viable prospect for Western social scientists for the first time in over seventy years. As a scholar interested in Asian populations, social change, and dance, I found the former Soviet Republic of Uzbekistan a fascinating research site. With a population of some twenty million, it was by far the largest of the former Soviet Muslim Central Asian republics. It was also likely to be significant internationally because of its wealth of natural resources, most notably oil, gold, and arable land. Uzbekistan also has a rich and complex historical legacy because its territory was located on the Silk Road and contained the legendary cities of Samarkand and Bukhara.

As for dance, I found two provocative references in the works of Mary Grace Swift (1968: 179–182) and Gregory Massell (1974). Swift gave a brief capsule history of Tamara Khonim, the first woman in Uzbekistan to dance unveiled in public. According to Swift, the first dancers in Uzbekistan were highly controversial figures in Soviet programs to encourage Uzbek women to abandon Muslim practices such as veiling. One of the

early dancers in Khonim's troupe was murdered by her brother for dancing in public. How could performing lead to violence? Why would women
risk their lives to dance?

Massell (1974: 175n., 239–244) said that the Soviet state used the performing arts to publicize programs to enlist women as a "surrogate proletariat" in Central Asia. How did the Soviet state use the expressive arts
as tools of social change? Did everyday gestures and kinetic practices become significant bases of a new national identity? Did the Soviet government attempt to create a new national consciousness through embodied
knowledge? If so, how? What impacts did participating in Soviet arts programs have on individual dancers, and in turn, how did Uzbek artists
shape national dance? These questions became the focus of my long-term
field research.

Acknowledgments

I am deeply grateful to many individuals and organizations for their assistance with this study. Alexia Bloch, Richard Davis, Bruce Grant, Michael Herzfeld, Philip Kilbride, Christine Koggel, Stephan Miescher, Janet Monge, Jane Plitt, Nancy Ries, Azade Seyhan, and Cynthia Werner offered encouragement, helpful advice, and fresh perspectives; and Nilufar Egamberdieva helped with translations. This manuscript also benefited from the thoughtful comments of two anonymous reviewers. Indiana University faculty, especially my advisor Anya Peterson Royce, and dissertation committee members Scott Alexander, Joelle Bahloul, Carol Greenhouse, and Ruth Stone were invaluable in shaping and realizing this project. Khayrulla H. Ismatulla introduced me to the beauty of the Uzbek language. Margaret Craske, George Tomal, Floris Alexander, Garth Fagan and members of the Garth Fagan Dance Theater, Stefa Zawerucha, Roziya Karimova, and Brian Gallagher shared rich and diverse visions of dance. Linda Zook, Ginger Goyer, Bernadette Pace, Lonny Dolin, Gulsara Dostova, Terri Murphy, and my parents have graced the journey with their friendship, humor, and support. The editorial staff at Greenwood Publishing Group, Inc.—Jane Garry, Acquisitions Editor; Leanne Small, Assistant Manager for Editorial Administration; Heidi Straight, Production Editor; and Debi McNeil of A&B Typesetters, copy editor—have shepherded this project through publication with perception and care. To the institutes, artists, and individuals in the Republic of Uzbekistan who opened their classrooms, studios, homes and hearts to a total stranger from a distant place, *mehmondarchilingiz, yordamingiz, katta rahmat*.

Generous funding from the Indiana University Skomp Fund, the Indiana University Center for Global Change and World Peace, IREX and the National Science Foundation made my research possible. Finally, I wish to thank the Social Science Research Council, Barbara Anderson, Nancy

Tuma, Michael Kennedy, Marjorie Mandelstam Balzer, Leyla Neyzi, and all of the scholars who participated in a very stimulating series of dissertation workshops to assist junior researchers entering the field of post-Soviet studies.

Note on Transliteration

Uzbek was written in a modified Cyrillic alphabet through most of the Soviet period. The Uzbek government recently adopted a new, Latin alphabet to replace Cyrillic. For ease of comprehension, I have chosen to transliterate Uzbek following the conventions Khayrulla H. Ismatulla provides in his Uzbek-English textbook, *Modern Literary Uzbek* (1995: 1–2). Some sounds in Uzbek have no counterparts in English. To give the reader a rough idea, I include my impressions of them below in parentheses. Russian speakers will find some of the words in the text familiar. Many Uzbek speakers, especially in the capital city of Tashkent, use words borrowed or adapted from Russian. These words appear as my interview partners used them and are transliterated employing Ismatulla's conventions for Uzbek.

ö has no counterpart in English (a rounder version of the sound "Awww")

q indicates a sound made in the back of the throat (like the "k" in "caw")

gh has no counterpart in English (I practiced gargling to learn it)

kh indicates a "ch" (as in "Bach")

Introduction

The occasion was *iftar*, an evening feast held during the holy month of Ramadan. I was attending as the American friend of a couple, Marat[1] and Mohira, who were members of the intelligentsia. I followed Mohira's broad back, encased in a heavy black coat, and looked at her dainty pointed black boots clipping staunchly along the slushy sidewalk. My own feet were cold, wet and sticky in boots from a Tashkent shop. Glue holding the boots together melted and ran into my socks whenever I wore them. Marat pointed out a graveyard to the right where his parents were buried. We were on our way to visit Marat's brothers who shared a compound on the outskirts of Tashkent. I had only arrived in Uzbekistan a month before and was delighted to be included in a family occasion.

The house was guarded, like most, by a high wall and was entered through a heavy gate of solid metal. A group of women and children surged out of the open gate to greet us murmuring, *"Qalaysiz"* (How are you?) and *"Yakhshi keling"* (Welcome) in soft voices. Mohira and the women embraced by standing face to face, grasping each other's elbows, right hand to the other's left elbow, and left hand to the other's right elbow. After a moment's hesitation and slightly startled glances, our hostesses touched my elbows too but kept as much distance as possible between their bodies and mine. I felt very much an outsider, although I appreciated the effort the women made to welcome me. Mohira paused to hug two young girls leaning out the window.

Our hostesses led us through the gate into a courtyard bordered by walls and doors. The compound was built in a rectangle, composed of strings of rooms forming the sides of the courtyard. I caught a brief glimpse into a cramped kitchen lit by yellow light in the middle of the yard as our hostesses led Mohira and me to rooms on the right. Marat did not come with us, and I did not see him again until it was time to leave.

Slipping off our shoes at the doorsill, we entered a room with a long, low table covered with tiny bowls and dishes filled with delicacies. An elderly lady sat at the head of the table. Behind her was a cabinet with glass doors filled with photographs and china. To her left were small tables with a telephone and a television. As we entered, she heaved herself painfully to her feet to embrace Mohira. Wrinkled, bent, smiling, and nearly toothless, she hugged me warmly although we had never met before. For the first time since crossing the threshold of this house, I relaxed. Mohira and I sat near the head of the table at the old woman's right-hand side. We rested on quilts laid on the floor, with cushions to support our backs.

The profusion of dishes on the table was overwhelming: triangles and half circles of crisp pastry filled with minced lamb or grated pumpkin (*qowoq*), flat golden rounds of bread (*non*), white fluff, yogurt cream, nuts, black raisins, yellow cake with chocolate icing, thin oily pancakes folded into quarters, and candies wrapped in twists of paper. The women at the table gestured, inviting me to eat. I knew that during the month of Ramadan observant Muslims do not eat or drink from sunup to sundown. I looked out the window and saw that dusk had not yet fallen. I shook my head and sensed approval and a slight thaw from the other women. We waited together until sundown to begin the feast.

Young and middle-aged women entered, alone or in groups of two or three. I watched Mohira and the other women at the table carefully for etiquette. Each time a new person came, we all stood and greeted the newcomer, embracing with hands briefly touching the other's elbows, then seated ourselves again. By the time seven or eight women had entered, I felt like a jack-in-the-box and my knees and legs ached from repeatedly rising and sinking to the floor.

When about ten of us ringed the table, the elderly lady rapidly mumbled under her breath, while everyone silently gazed down into cupped hands. I caught only the last word in each phrase— . . . *tursin* (may you stay) . . . *bölsin* (may you be). As her voice rose to an emphatic close, everyone whispered a phrase, raised their cupped hands to their faces, then swept their hands over their foreheads and cheeks as though rinsing them with water.

Another very elderly lady entered, her hair improbably black and her lips an eye-catching carnation pink. She had bright blue eyes, although one was clouded with white tissue. Assisted by one of the younger women, the first elderly lady rose to her feet to greet the newcomer, then tottered out of the room. The elderly lady with blue eyes took over the head of the table.

Mohira was asked to recite the Quran. She recited a portion of a *sura* (chapter), her clear voice rising and falling, bringing out each syllable of the rhythmic phrases. Two more women recited long sections as well, followed by two or three short recitations. The women began checking their watches. Finally, at fifteen minutes after six our hostesses brought pots of tea into the room. Guests who had been fasting all day gingerly sipped water.

"*Oling, oling*" (eat, eat, or literally, take, take). People urged food on each other and on me, proffering dishes, even plopping things on my plate. I made a careful mental inventory of dishes on the table, knowing I would want to list them later in my field notes. We started with the crisp pastries filled with meat or squash (*somsa*). I recognized the *somsa* Mohira had made the day before. We had spent the afternoon in her kitchen while I grated chunks of orange squash with dark green skins (*qowoq*), and she rolled out fragile circles of dough. With pride I noticed that hers were the prettiest on the plates of *somsa* scattered around the table. Women turned over the *somsa* with quick, assessing glances, before biting into them. I saw that some were burnt black on the bottom, while others were golden brown.

A sweet white fluff that tasted like marshmallow was a great favorite. The women tore chunks off flat chewy rounds of bread and dipped them into the fluff. The bread seemed all the same to me, but Mohira told me there were three different kinds on the table, each with a special name. The only differences I could find were in the markings pricked into the rounds: some had crosshatches and others had circles.

We ate until I thought I would not be able to stand up. A meat broth filled with bits of meat and shaved noodles was followed by two kinds of *dolma*, one made with grape leaves stuffed with ground meat and rice and the other with cabbage leaves. Using their fingers, the women ate every bit of the heaps of oily shaved noodles with bits of horse meat (*norin*). The dish was a great delicacy and very difficult to make because cutting the noodles into fine slivers was a very time-consuming process. I tried to look pleased too, although I knew *norin* was so heavy that my stomach would ache all night. The final course was kebabs, savory ground meat shaped into dainty oblongs the size of my thumb and grilled on skewers.

While we ate, the women chatted. One woman challenged the wording of one line of Mohira's recitation of the Quran. Mohira responded graciously but firmly. After a bit more discussion, the women decided to consult a text. Someone came to the door from the courtyard and handed in a book. Squinting at the page, the challenger sent a child for her glasses. The point was settled, and the challenger thanked Mohira, who seemed to have won the genteel debate. I sensed that rather than an occasion of commensality, this gathering was a nuanced and highly competitive game. I wondered if the tensions I sensed were common among women, or particular to this group of relatives.

Conversation turned to families. Each woman asked every other woman in the room after the well-being of relatives, children, and grandchildren, by name. The questions and answers were a smooth, rapid litany:

And how is your daughter Halima?
Thank you, thanks be to God.
And how is your granddaughter Kamila?
Thank you, thanks be to God.

After a woman managed a particularly long string of inquiries, a victorious glint flashed in her eyes at the feat of memory. Mohira received condolences on a recent death in her family. Although I was a stranger, I was included with hesitant questions after my parents (Well, thanks be to God) and my children (None). Again I felt my isolation from the tight web of relationships linking the other women at the table, and the polite puzzlement of the women.

Talk drifted to prices. One family was assembling a dowry. A woman discussed the price of a Bukharan carpet her family had just purchased for the bride. Although she expressed shock about the rapid increase in prices, her face bore a triumphant, if somewhat pained, smile.

Mohira introduced me as her guest. "She is a Japanese girl, but from America. Her father is a big professor of sociology. On his birthday, she sent him a computer letter. She concerns herself with national people's dances and is writing a book about them." Mohira had been distant, even cool, to everyone but the first very elderly lady and to the children. I sensed that she stressed my foreign origin, academic family, access to technology, and education as a way of affirming and adding to her own status. I wondered why Mohira wanted to display me like an exotic bird. She was very successful professionally. Why did she feel the need for additional affirmation among her husband's relatives? Even though it was unusual to tell a guest to bring gifts, she had told me to bring lots of American candy to this *iftar* "for the children." Since even local sugar and candy were quite costly for the average Uzbek budget, our hostesses received the imported candy with eyebrows raised in impressed surprise. While bringing me to the *iftar* celebration was indeed a gracious kindness to me as a visitor, it also seemed that I was a counter in the game between Mohira and the other women.

Shortly after we finished the last course, Mohira requested permission to leave, saying that the buses stopped at eight P.M. One of the older ladies murmured another long rhythmic series of sentences, perhaps a blessing, which all received with cupped hands. As we left, I saw several teenage girls working in the courtyard kitchen. Our hostesses huddled in the chilly February weather in kerchiefs, faded print housedresses, and layers of sweaters. Their noses were bright red and they looked quite exhausted and miserable. They had spent only a brief time at the feast. I realized with a guilty pang that they had labored in the cold, cooking, fetching pots of tea, and serving course after course while we dined like queens. I looked at Mohira, resplendent in a warm, elegant coat and boots, and saw that a huge disparity existed between her, a member of the intelligentsia, and her in-laws.

Mohira had pursued education and a profession during the Soviet period, and continued her work after independence. Although I had no opportunity to speak with Mohira's in-laws because they had been in the kitchen all day, they seemed to have taken the more traditional Central Asian route of domesticity. They cooked while a horde of children played in the courtyard. From their worn clothing and thin bodies, they appeared far less affluent than Mohira. I realized that several of the women were actually much younger than I had thought at first. Chapped faces and hunched postures had given them the appearance of middle age. Participation in public life had brought Mohira material comfort, education, recognition, and confidence. Domesticity seemed to have given her female in-laws limited means, strained health, fatigue, and many children.

HOST AND GUEST

The courtesy Marat's relatives showed me exemplified the frame that would dominate every interaction that occurred during my field research in Uzbekistan: the relationship between host and guest. This norm of hospitality governed every transaction, from purchasing items in stores, asking directions, conducting interviews, meeting neighbors, or making friends. Whatever other dynamics affected these relationships, I was always first and foremost a *mehmon*, a guest. Being a *mehmon* meant that I was allowed to make faux pas, while those I met were supposed to offer help and hospitality. Doing so acknowledged and added to the stature of my host and to me as a guest of the country. At the very least, no request I made could directly be refused. People constantly referred to me as the *mehmon*.

Guests have a special status in Uzbekistan. When I thanked people for assistance or hospitality, they frequently responded with the aphorisms "Guests are gifts from God," meaning helping a visitor was a sacred duty and their efforts would be rewarded many times over. Another frequent response was "A guest comes before even your father," in other words, as hosts they should give me every welcome possible. Thus, although gender, age, appearance, and the purpose of this project were all factors in the interview, the paramount frame was the relationship between host and guest.

The *iftar* celebration provided a point of departure into understanding Uzbek hospitality. The guests did not lift a finger to help the busy hostesses. The modest household that treated us to a lavish feast almost cer-

tainly went hungry to feed us. Such feasts were a common event in
Uzbekistan. Holidays, birthdays, weddings, and "teas" were other occasions
when I enjoyed elaborate entertainment.

Visitors to Uzbekistan quickly discover that an invitation to *choy* (tea) is
a memorable experience. "Tea" is a lengthy meal in a private home, usually requiring at least a full day of labor by several women. Upon arrival,
guests are seated at a table covered by a tablecloth and an overwhelming
array of small dishes of nuts, candies, raisins, and fresh fruit. At most of
the teas I attended, male and female guests sat at the same table. The
host, usually the male head of the household, tore flat rounds of *non* into
fragments and scattered them around the table. The hostess perched
briefly at the table to pour the first of many rounds of tea into small china
bowls (*piyolalar*) or placed someone near the head of the table in charge
of the teapot.

The women in the household worked in the kitchen, emerging to clear
the table and to serve the next course. Tea usually consisted of three or
more courses, beginning with *shorba* (a soup of lamb, carrots, onions, and
potatoes), followed by second or even third courses such as steamed
dumplings (*manti*) or stuffed grape leaves (*dolma*). The final course was
always *palov*, a steaming platter of rice boiled with sauteed lamb, carrots,
onions, cumin, and garlic. Fruit in season, perhaps a melon, completed
the meal. Guests left shortly after eating the last bite.

Standing in the vestibule, host and guests pressed gifts on each other
after polite refusals. The women who had worked so hard in the kitchen
would finally come out to say good-bye and accept well deserved compli-
ments on their hard work. Men might receive a shirt, a dark green and
white embroidered cap (*döppi*), or a gilt-handled knife with a steel blade
(*pichoq*). People gave me gifts appropriate for women: dress lengths of
atlas (the national fabric of silk dyed in multicolored ikat patterns) or a
döppi embroidered with gold thread. I usually gave imported candy and a
plastic shopping bag from an American store filled with small items such
as lipsticks, pens, and notepads. I would hand the bag to the hostess so
she could dole out items to household members later.

As I became more familiar with the cost of living, I realized that the
meal and gifts were a substantial burden on a household's resources. A
dress length of *atlas* alone cost one to two weeks' salary. Why did people
engage in such lavish hospitality? An invitation to tea was an investment
in a potentially long-standing relationship between host and guest. Giving
gifts as a way to initiate a relationship (Malinowski [1922] 1984) or to
enhance the prestige of the donor (Mauss 1967: 37–39) are familiar
themes in anthropology. Like a Kula armband or a potlatch, tea in Uzbekistan honored both donor and recipient and affirmed the bond between them. Months and even years later, people would refer with pride
and satisfaction to the occasion when someone was a guest in their home.

During tea or soon afterward, people often began to explore mutually beneficial exchanges. For example, over tea one hostess asked me to be on the board of an international women's organization she wanted to found, and to make a contribution to the organization. I learned to be careful about accepting lavish hospitality until I knew what my potential hosts might hope to gain from our relationship. I did not want anyone to invest a substantial portion of the household resources with unrealistic expectations of my resources.

Especially during my first visit in 1992, I was often the first American an individual had ever met. People were uncertain what I might be able to do, and had oddly skewed notions of American life based on American television series such as *Santa Barbara*. I encountered requests as modest as a few aspirin, due to an absolute dearth of reliable medicines after Uzbekistan declared independence from the Soviet Union. Requests for English lessons for children were frequent. At the other end of the spectrum, a few people asked if I could send one of their children to America for a college education. I also had to be careful not to give more than a token souvenir such as a postcard too soon, lest the recipient feel unduly obligated to meet my next request.

By 1994, several years of encounters with foreigners had led Tashkent residents to more realistic expectations and greater caution about extending hospitality. In rural areas I visited, I continued to encounter the open hospitality I had encountered in 1992.

Erving Goffman ([1974] 1986: 10) developed the notion of "frame" for categories of social events and the "principles of organization" governing different kinds of interactions. Uzbeks often applied the frame of hospitality to situations I was accustomed to thinking of in terms of a contract for buying goods or hiring labor. For instance, through friends I arranged to stay in an apartment. I thought that I was renting the apartment, for an appropriate sum of money. I was quite disconcerted to walk in and find my "landlady" having tea and a snack in the kitchen with another woman. Although I had given her money to live there, she thought that she was still free to come and go in the apartment. I learned that she thought of herself not as a landlady, but as a hostess. Anything I gave her, including money, was simply a gift from a guest. As a guest, I was supposed to happily accept whatever accommodations she graciously allowed me.

I suspect that this difference in interpretation was due in large part to the fact that we were used to two different economic systems. According to one Uzbek acquaintance, the government provided housing until independence. Thereafter, people could own their own residences and could buy and sell them. Thus, the notion of renting, buying or selling housing was still relatively new in 1994. I was used to a capitalist economy, with the notions of contract such as leases and exchange of rights or goods for money. My "hostess," on the other hand, had probably received housing as an entitlement from the government most of her life. The notion of renting an apartment seemed wholly unfamiliar to her. She applied the more familiar "frame" of hospitality to define the relationship with me, a foreigner and a stranger staying in her home. Through a friend who had arranged for me to stay in her apartment, we untangled the misunderstanding and I began looking for other quarters.

The frame of host and guest, although often heartwarming, could and did leave me in a position of almost total dependence on the choices and generosity of my hosts. Polite guests do not complain, and should be delighted with whatever is offered. While these norms were appropriate for occasions such as tea, they could be quite disconcerting as a paradigm for transactions I thought of as commercial exchanges. I learned, however, to be aware that situations I would view as contractual exchanges in the United States might be interpreted as an exchange of gifts in Uzbekistan, leaving me with no recourse but hope that my host's inclinations would coincide with mine.

The relationships forged through hospitality also served as an entree into a network of information and access to scarce goods. With erratic means of supply for consumer goods, individuals were largely dependent on an informal network of relatives and friends for obtaining scarce items. Hospitality often initiated membership into a loose but critical web of information about where one could find butter today, or an opportunity to share in a lucky purchase of honey. It also provided occasions for buying items. At one bridal party I attended, women huddled in a corner to examine goods one of the guests had recently brought back from a trip to Iran.

Hospitality was such an important aspect of Uzbek life that Jamila, a young woman who grew up in a rural village, identified it as essential to being Uzbek:

MD: What does it mean to be Uzbek?

Jamila: Uzbek people have a broad hug [gesturing wide with her arms, then miming a hug]. I think you have met mostly Tashkent Uzbeks. The system has changed them. They have become [clenching her fist and squeezing] . . . They are not like others. If someone lives in Tashkent for a long time, then comes back, they will say "You have become dry" [*Quruq bölib tursan*]. Lots of talk, "Oh, come, you must be my guest" but no meaning. But elsewhere, even if people have not enough food, they will say come be my guest. They are happy to see guests—they will say you have been like a river—while we have been here. "What is happening?" They like to talk.

GENDER AND COLONIALISM

The *iftar* celebration was also a microcosm of relationships and issues that shaped my fieldwork in Uzbekistan. It embodied a map of fundamental distinctions constituting social order. As we entered, the men went to the left of the compound and women went to the right, marking the acutely segregated nature of relationships between men and women. During the day at Marat's house, I did not see the men again until we were saying good-bye at the gate to the street, so I do not know what occurred at the men's observation of the holiday.

Returning to the women's celebration of *iftar* at Mohira's in-laws, hierarchies based on seniority were clear. The oldest women sat at the head of the table, with guests seated in descending order by age. Older guests sat nearest the head of the table and youngest by the foot. Women were also extremely competitive. Baking, dowries for prospective brides, memory of family connections, and knowledge of the Quran served as arenas of delicately pointed combat.

Both Mohira and her husband had attended universities during the Soviet period and rose to prominent positions for their intellectual achievements. I had seen Mohira with friends and colleagues who were also members of the intelligentsia. She was warm and outgoing, greeting people with a gracious smile. I was surprised and puzzled by the tense formality of Mohira's interactions with her in-laws. Our hostesses seemed both to admire and envy her, while she seemed to hide a touch of disdain behind a veneer of exquisitely formal manners.

Perhaps the unease between Mohira and her in-laws had a particular history, but seeing such disparate women together made me wonder how the Soviet period changed the lives of women. With her education, carefully applied makeup, career, and costly European clothing, Mohira looked almost alien among the tired, gaunt women in their ragged housedresses and head scarves. Had the Soviets created or enabled radically different ways of life for women? Who had participated in the Soviet programs? What had been the individual consequences of doing so? These issues about the impact of the Soviet period on women suggested the broader social context and implications of my research.

GENDER, KINSHIP, AND NATIONALISM

Jane Cowan (1990) studied how dance events embody gender hierarchies and other political relationships in a Greek community. George Mosse (1985) looked at the rise of bourgeois morality in relation to the rise of nationalism in Germany and other European nations. He argued that notions of "respectability" legitimized the rising middle class. Nationalist ideologies co-opted and elaborated ideals of masculinity and femininity, and male and female beauty. Brackette Williams (1996: 3) asked:

How are different concepts, categories and practices, . . . assimilated to nationalist movements? How do these assimilations assist or hinder the consolidation of the

Mustaqillik Maydoni (Independence Square), Tashkent, on Independence Day (September 1) in 1994.

constellations of ideas and practices referred to as nationalism? How are prior divisions, such as gender, age, caste and class implicated in the generation of criteria for citizenship, loyalty and the legitimacy of social actions statistically or stereotypically associated with status classification?

Uzbek national dances intersect these discussions in several ways. I explore interrelationships among dance, gender, and nationalism. Broadly, I ask how kinship idioms and related notions about gender figure into the ways the state promoted and shaped a national identity, first in the Soviet period, and later during independence.[2] More specifically, I argue that dancers, as symbolic "girls" or unmarried females in the Uzbek kinship system, were effective symbolic mediators between extended kin groups and the Uzbek nation-state. National dances and dancing provided an expressive form and a social space for constructing and representing notions of "Uzbek" as a collective identity.

METHODS AND DATA

The capital city of Tashkent is a sprawling metropolis with a population of some two million people. Since it is also the center of the Uzbek professional dance world, I spent the majority of my time in Tashkent. Although there is a charming neighborhood of low, clay buildings and narrow, winding streets known as the "Old City" in Tashkent, most of the buildings I saw looked contemporary. Downtown Tashkent has wide,

A *howli.*

paved avenues with multiple lanes of aggressive automobile drivers. Sleek, tall buildings border green parks with brass monuments. The subway system (metro) is a showcase. Each subway stop is distinct, with murals, bas-relief portraits of astronauts, or vaulted ceilings with star-patterned mosaics in shades of blue. A network of trams and buses extends transportation to outlying residential neighborhoods.

Tashkentese live in multistory apartment buildings or in compounds called *howlis*. The apartments are usually homes for a nuclear family of parents, children, and perhaps a single relative such as a niece or mother. Extended families consisting of parents, unmarried children, and married sons and their wives and children, on the other hand, share a *howli*. A *howli* is a single-story dwelling consisting of strings of rooms built around a courtyard. The courtyard usually has a vegetable garden, grapevines, and fruit trees. In warm weather a family takes meals outside on a raised platform called an *aywon*. When a son in the family marries, he and his bride receive one or more rooms as private quarters. All of the homes I visited in Tashkent had cold running water, electricity, and gas. Apartments had indoor plumbing and hot water as well. Some but not all of the *howlis* I visited had hot water.

I made brief trips to four major cities and three rural areas. At the regional and local levels amateur performing groups were also very active. I gathered some information on these groups but a systematic study of them was severely hampered by difficulties with travel outside the capital during 1994. Legal requirements for trips inside Uzbekistan were unsettled during much of my stay so I decided to concentrate my research on professional dancers in Tashkent rather than try to divide my time between Tashkent and another region like Bukhara or Khorezm.

To look beyond the printed history of women and national dances in Uzbekistan, I used life histories and dance ethnography as principal fieldwork methods. I gathered about twenty life and career histories of dancers to explore the actual impact of Soviet gender policies at the individual level. A few individuals were kind enough to spend two or three sessions with me over several weeks; other interviews were as brief as fifteen minutes during a rehearsal break. Most of the conversations were a single session of forty-five minutes to an hour. The ages of the individuals I interviewed ranged from about twelve to seventy, so the life histories give this study a chronological span from the early years of Soviet rule in Central Asia (circa 1924) through Uzbekistan's political independence (1991) and the period of my extended field research (1994).

In addition to biographical and autobiographical accounts, I made videotapes of dances shown on television and filmed live performances and rehearsals using a portable video camera. Uzbek friends also gave me several additional videotapes about Uzbek dance as handsome gifts. In addition, I engaged in participant observation and limited archival research.

LIFE HISTORIES

Professional national dancers were an ideal group for examining the impact of Soviet reforms on women's lives because professional national dance developed during the Soviet regime. Prior to the Soviet period, women did not dance in public. Dance as a profession was a highly visible measure that flew in the face of indigenous Muslim norms about the modest conduct expected of women. Dance was so controversial that many of the earliest dancers were orphans, selected and trained by the state. Due to the visible and controversial nature of their profession, dancers were directly confronted with the tensions and contradictions between Soviet and Muslim norms. While the Soviet programs to introduce women into the workplace were aimed at many individuals in many other professions, the dancers presented a very clear-cut and dramatic example.

For comparison I elicited some fifteen life histories of individuals in other professions, in both urban and rural areas. These individuals ranged in age from sixteen to seventy. Most of these interviews were with women.

Most of the dancers I talked with were performing, or used to perform, in one of the five major national dance companies in Tashkent. Dancers in the Tashkent companies were at the pinnacle of the professional dance field, thus the sample is weighted toward the most successful professional dancers. Within this pool, I spoke to both well-known soloists and members of the corps.

Tashkent was the hub of professional dance training and performance. The most promising children from all over the country came to Tashkent to study at choreographic schools. Upon graduation, students of an institute join a professional dance company or return to the provinces to teach. In 1994, all the graduates of the *maktab* (school) who I met joined three of the five major dance companies in Tashkent. In fact the demand for dancers was so great in 1994, the companies in Tashkent hired the graduating class and took the next year's graduating class a year early.

In addition to the professional companies in Tashkent, there were professional and amateur regional companies. During visits to three regions, I interviewed directors of regional dance companies, one amateur company for children, and one professional company of young adults. I also spoke with adult participants in a competition for amateur adult folk dancers and singers.

During the interviews I asked about geographic origin, family members, siblings, occupations of parents and siblings, and the individual's age and marital status. I chose these questions because they were the questions nearly every Uzbek I met immediately asked me. I broadly indicated the kind of information I was looking for, and my interview partner[3] would look relieved, exhale, and launch into a relaxed, rapid monologue for ten or fifteen minutes.

Having established the important facts, according to Uzbek conversational conventions, the talk would turn to dance. With a bit of prompting from me, we would discuss how the individual chose dance as a profession, parental response, childhood exposure to dance, training, employment history, and aspirations for the future. Interviews thus traced the major "givens" and turning points that shape an Uzbek woman's life—family and place of origin, choice of profession, marriage, and motherhood. We discussed how she managed, or would like to resolve, conflicts, if any, between her career and her family. I taped most of the interviews, explaining that I still needed a dictionary for many words and this way I could look them up later.

Uzbeks usually asked me my ethnic origin, probably because I am Japanese-American and, based on my appearance, could belong to several Central Asian ethnic groups. I noticed that asking my interview partner questions about her ethnicity often caused an embarrassed flush, so I did not ask this question unless the person was very relaxed and forthcoming.

Dancers who were *mestis* (a combination of Uzbek and another ethnic group, usually Tatar or Russian) seemed to be the most uncomfortable with this question. Uzbek men often married Russian or Tatar women. Uzbek women, however, virtually always married Uzbek men. I noticed that women with Tatar or Russian mothers frequently had Russian first

names and Uzbek last names. Coloring provided another clue, although
it was not always reliable. People with a Russian or Tatar parent or grandparent often had light-colored eyes. Blond or auburn hair was also common. On the other hand, those descended from Tajiks or Uzbeks on both
sides of the family tended to have brown eyes and very dark brown or
black hair.

We often talked in dressing rooms or theaters during breaks or idle
moments of rehearsals. Sometimes we had relative privacy in an empty
corner, backstage, or in the seats for the audience. Other discussions took
place in groups or with a curious, slightly envious audience of other dancers. A few longer interviews occurred over lunch or coffee before or after
rehearsal; interviews with retired dancers took place in their homes or
places where they worked in their second careers. I attended rehearsals
over a period of five months, so most participants knew me at least by
sight for at least several weeks before I requested an interview. Most people were pleased and flattered at being invited to participate.

Lewis Langness and Gelya Frank (1981) noted verification as one of the
major difficulties with using life histories. My primary focus in these life
histories was how these individuals interpreted their experiences as dancers during the Soviet years and in the rapidly changing climate of independence. I wanted to hear the dancers' perspectives, so verification was
a secondary concern. Nevertheless I gathered biographical information
and interviews with dancers published in periodicals and books from the
Soviet decades (1930–1990) to compare with the oral accounts I recorded
in 1994. I also gathered comments about dancers from other dancers and
members of the general public.

DATA OR NARRATIVE?

Life histories provide scholars with a host of interpretive choices. James
Peacock and Dorothy Holland's (1993) thoughtful overview sets up a basic
choice in analyzing life histories. The life history can be a source of information about events in the past, or it can be a construction of the
speaker's self. "At one extreme, the narration is only a mirror of reality;
at the other, the narration is the reality" (1993: 371). These poles are not
mutually exclusive; for example, Susan Rodgers (1995) viewed autobiographies of men who grew up in colonial Indonesia as lenses revealing both
the development of their individual awareness and broader social and
political developments. Rodgers argued that "telling a life unavoidably
also involves telling history in terms of passages through ages of time and
transitions between levels of consciousness and social awareness" (1995:
3).

Thus, in placing this study on the continuum between "objective" data
and "subjective" narrative, I offer it principally as a collection of individual

women's recollections of their lives and careers as dancers. Their life histories contain valuable and difficult to obtain information about events, institutions, and experiences that occurred during the Soviet period. Although I recognize that this information is mediated through the memories and sensibilities of the individual speakers, I also discuss these historical developments as they are visible through the retrospective gaze of my interview partners.

Like Rodgers (1995: 3) I argue that there is an intersection between personal history and social history.[4] Juxtaposing the life histories in this study reveals the unfolding of profound changes in consciousness during seventy years of Soviet rule, from obedient child to self-sufficient professional and from Muslim Central Asian to Soviet citizen.

Another issue I faced as an author was how to present the life histories. Marjorie Shostak in her well-known study of Nisa, a !Kung woman ([1981] 1983), separated discussion of ethnographic issues from Nisa's accounts of her life, and foregrounded lengthy sections of conversations with Nisa. At the other end of the spectrum, Mary Catherine Bateson (1993) paraphrased life histories and drew from them to discuss particular themes. A third alternative would be to intersperse quotations from interviews with comments and observations (see, e.g., Belinda Bozzoli 1991). I have chosen to use the third approach in order to amplify information from the life histories with data from dances, archives, and participant-observation.

Peacock and Holland (1993) also problematize the production of a particular narrative. Life histories are products of a particular time, place, and relationship. In this study they are conversations held in 1992 or 1994 with me over a tape recorder. In working with the life histories in this study, I wanted to present them in the spirit in which people shared them with me, that is, what did participating in interviews mean to my partners?

Richard Bauman (1977) suggested that scholars study verbal art as performance. He identified performance as "a mode of language use, a way of speaking" (1977: 11). Speakers could "key" listeners that they were switching from informal conversation to verbal performance through formal devices such as parallel grammatical constructions and changing vocal intonation (1977: 18–20).

Comparing formal aspects of the life histories with other kinds of oral speech in Uzbekistan suggested that the life histories were reflexive and delicately crafted performances. As my interview partners told me about their experiences, they drew on a repertoire of forms of oral communication. The presence of the tape recorder usually triggered an immediate change from conversational speech into a different mode of speech, which I shall refer to as "formal" speech. People spoke more loudly and slowly. Men would speak emphatically, sometimes with a ringing tone. Women lowered their voices about half an octave and adopted a velvety timbre that reminded me of the American actress Ann Margret. As people warmed to their subject, they would often slip into a rhythmic, repetitive syntax.

While writing this study and listening to recordings of interviews, I recognized where else I had heard people speak in a similar way. The cadences and syntax of formal speech greatly resembled classical poetry recitations and speeches given at weddings. Poetry is a beloved art in Uzbekistan. Uzbeks take great pride in Central Asian poets. Alisher Navoi (1441–1501), for example, was a beloved historical figure. In 1994, contemporary male and female poets were prominent and respected individuals. The leader of the Opposition Party *Erk* (freedom) was the male poet Muhammad Solih. The female national poet Oydin Hojaeva was elected to Parliament just before I left in 1994.

I saw poetry recitation frequently on television. Poets appeared on talk shows to read their poetry. Professional emcees used a few lines of verse to set the stage for the next performer in televised variety concerts. Vocal timbre and cadence set the poetic speech off from conversational speech. Male voices were smooth and clear; female voices were deep and soft. The day after I arrived was the poet Navoi's birthday (February 8). In the gloomy winter weather, a line of little girls with enormous fluffy chiffon bows on their heads stood in front of a monument to Navoi and recited in shrill voices. I could not understand what they said, but the rhythm of the words was as even as a metronome. Some of the children even rocked slightly in time to the words.

Formal speech occurred in social settings as well. At weddings, a steady stream of friends and relatives would step up to a microphone in front of hundreds of guests to salute the happy couple with a smooth outpouring of wishes for their happiness, health, and prosperity. Speakers appeared delighted and showed no signs of anxiety. The booming microphone and teeming audience seemed merely to add to their pleasure. The bride and groom stood with heads respectfully bowed to receive the good wishes. Guests usually ignored the speaker and continued to eat, drink, and chat with other people seated at the same table.

Wedding salutations provided a clear example of the sentence structures that distinguished formal speech from conversational speech. A brief explanation of Uzbek grammar is necessary. Uzbek is an agglutinative language that places verbs at the end of a sentence. It is easy to establish a steady pulse and repetitive rhyme scheme in Uzbek because most verbs (in the same person) have the same final syllable. For example, formal speech wishing newlyweds happiness and tranquillity falls into a rhyme as follows:

Bakhtli bölsin! (Happy may you be!)

Tinchlik bölsin! (Peaceful may you be!)

By contrast, in conversational speech people usually used sentence structures and verbal forms that produced a more staggered rhythm. Speech, at least in the Tashkent dialect with which I am most familiar, ranged from clipped sentences like *"Ketdik!"* (Let's go!) to extended complex sentences such as *"Ishga borib, Kazakstandan kelgan ayol kishini kurib, uyiga kaitib keldim"* (Having gone to work and having seen the woman who came from Kazakstan, I came back to the house).

People also used formal speech to toast guests invited to their homes for tea or for feasts such as a dissertation defense I attended. In daily life, introducing people to each other was also an occasion for lengthy and flattering descriptions. Exaggeration and hyperbole were the order of the day on such occasions.

Metaphors were a third marker of formal speech.[5] Throughout this study I present excerpts of interviews translated into English. I have tried to approximate literal meaning rather than using idioms more familiar to English speakers. The interviews I elicited were rich in vivid similes, but it is important to note that such phrases were common in formal speech. They were cues that the speaker was performing, and wanted eloquently to express profound and sincere emotion.

A love of beauty and ornamentation was evident in many aspects of Uzbek life from speech to dress to interior design. Pastoral images from nature were particular favorites. For example, many women's names began with the first syllable *Gul* (flower) or *Oy* (moon). Women prized barrettes studded with pearls and sweaters with glittering appliques. Multicolored painted arabesques and vines graced walls and ceilings in homes. Panels of plaster fretwork covered conference room walls. Everything had to be pretty (*chiroyli*). When a hostess asked me to make a table *chiroyli*, she wanted me to shake out the tablecloth, smooth it onto the table, and neatly arrange dishes and napkins. Young girls with sweet smiles and smooth round faces were *chiroyli*, as were red flowers, a graceful dancer, or a red pen with white lettering saying "Indiana University."

I also suspect that formal speech contained many literary allusions and may be an occasion for the speaker to demonstrate erudition and subtlety. My knowledge of Uzbek literature was inadequate to recognize most references. I did notice that my nickname "Mimi" drew frequent smiles. People often changed it to "Mimikhonim" to create a rhyming allusion to Bibikhonim, the Chinese princess who had married the Central Asian ruler Amur Timur (1336–1405). This was a witty reference to my Asian appearance with a touch of flattery because Bibikhonim was a historic figure. It may also have been a gentle gibe at my headstrong and career-oriented American ways. While her husband Amur Timur was away on a military campaign, Bibikhonim quickly (and, the implication is, willfully) authorized and built a great *madrasa* (place of study for Muslim scholars) before he returned.

A full exploration of the functions of poetry and of oral speech making is beyond the scope of this study. Nevertheless, in order to understand the spirit in which many people participated in interviews with me, it is important to appreciate the pleasure people took in speaking, and speaking well. Bauman (1977) noted the importance of understanding norms governing "competence" in verbal performance. In Uzbekistan, formal speaking was a fundamental skill necessary to participate in frequent and important social events such as weddings or teas. Based on characteristics of the language and the delivery style people used during the taped interviews, I conclude that the interviews were performative events like a television appearance or a wedding speech. They were self-conscious narratives, shaped by mastery of the idioms of public oral performance and an appreciation of Uzbek poetry.

Therefore, in deciding whether to present the life histories in this study as data from which to reconstruct past events or alternatively as oral narratives, I present them as I believe the speakers intended: as performances about their experiences as performers. The narratives do contain information of historical interest that I discuss from time to time. This study, however, is primarily about dancers' memories of the Soviet period and independence, rather than a social history.

If the life histories were performances, who was the intended audience? I was the immediate audience. Speakers also understood that I was writing a book about Uzbek dance and wanted to know about the lives of dancers. People in the United States would learn about them through reading what I wrote. In order to understand more fully the underlying dynamics of the interview process, however, it is necessary to recall the fundamental relationship discussed at the beginning of this introduction: host and guest.

The relationship of host and guest made people more willing to accommodate my requests for information, and proud to fulfill their obligations as hosts. It also accounts in part for the formal speech people used in the interviews. The speakers wanted to honor both me and themselves. Viewing our interactions within the Uzbek norms and practices of hospitality, I believe that people gave me their life histories as a gift from a *mezbon* (host) to a *mehmon* (guest). I see these narratives as gifts from the speakers to future readers. Since gifts also establish ties between donor and recipient, these narratives are tokens of friendship from Uzbek narrators to readers in the United States. My ethnographic role is that of intermediary—scribe, translator, and courier of these gifts of story.

DANCES AND DANCING

A second principal method I used was observing, learning, and videotaping dances. I present selected dances in this study as ethnographic records of artists' observations and experiences. This approach builds on the work of a number of scholars. Eric Hobsbawm (1983: 1) said "insofar as there is . . . reference to a historic past, the peculiarity of 'invented' traditions is that the continuity with it is largely factitious. . . . [T]hey are responses to novel situations which take the form of reference to old situations, or which establish their own past by quasi-obligatory repetition." He pointed out the difference between wholly new traditions, such as those created for the Boy Scouts, and older traditions that endure because people modify and adapt them (1983: 4).

Artists can be influential in the process of maintaining, creating, and adapting traditions. As Anya Peterson Royce's discussion (1993: 103–122) of the Isthmus Zapotec of Mexico demonstrated, Zapotec writers, musicians, dancers, sculptors, and painters help the Zapotec create and maintain a strongly marked ethnic identity within the context of Mexican society.

Turning to dance, the anthropology of dance is a relatively young subfield of anthropology. Scholars have looked at dance from various perspectives, including form and meaning (Royce 1984), strategies for defining ethnic identity (Royce 1982: 169–183), a semiotic system (Kaeppler 1977), and cultural constructions of gender (Cowan 1990).

Royce (1982: 168–183) demonstrated that social identities can be coded in dance. Her work among the Zapotec in Mexico showed how the Zapotec displayed skills in dances as a strategy for defining and maintaining a distinctive ethnic identity. For example, in a wedding between a Zapotec and a non-Zapotec, the Zapotec relatives may hire musicians to play the oldest kinds of music and request the women to wear lavish regional costumes (Royce 1977: 170). Royce (1991) explained the Zapotec notion of *guendalisaa* (creating community through dance, music, and celebration), which gives a central place of importance to dance. Participating in dance events (*velas*) sponsored by families established and maintained an individual's membership in the kin group and Zapotec community.

Sally Ann Ness (1992) unraveled the web of meanings associated with the *sinulog*, a ritual incorporating dance and prayer associated with Santo Nino in Cebu, a Philippine city. Cebu residents believed the *sinulog* had ancient origins. Ness identified a version considered "authentic" performed as a prayer to Santo Nino by women who sold candles. Her research also examined variants performed by male dance troupes founded at the beginning of the twentieth century. These male *sinulogs* became popular among prominent Cebu families. In 1980 professional dancers and choreographers created yet another kind of entertaining *sinulog* for parades. A local official asked artists to "revive" the *sinulog* to help develop a distinctive cultural identity for the region. The *sinulog* thus became a polyvalent symbol of faith, wealth, individual creativity, and local identity.

I am indebted to both Royce and Ness for providing frameworks and

methods for exploring the ways in which people construct, maintain, and
refine collective identities through dance and music. Royce (1982: 169–
183) explained how the Zapotec elaborated and manipulated a distinctive
style—symbols, dress, ceremonies, and values—as a strategy for marking
boundaries between ethnic groups. Ness (1992) showed how the "same"
symbol, the *sinulog*, continuously acquired new forms and meanings over
time.

Using the work of these two scholars as a point of departure, I chose
to examine Uzbek dance from the perspective of the dancers as active
and creative producers and reproducers of the art of Uzbek dance. I also
decided to take a diachronic approach to exploring the changing roles of
Uzbek dance and dancers from the early Soviet years through independence. I view the dances as a kind of narrative by artists. I analyze them
here as ethnographic registers of social change.

The methodological framework of this book is experimental. I designed
this project to explore Uzbek culture using three kinds of data: verbal
data from the dancers' life stories, visual and aural data from Uzbek
dances, and phenomenological data gathered from my own experiences
of learning the dances.

Would looking at life stories along with Uzbek dances provide a kind
of parallax? And what about learning some of the dances myself? What
can we learn about a society from studying dance and gesture? Is it appropriate to think of dance as analogous to verbal language, or is kinetic
expression different? If so, how? Are thought and action distinct in dance,
or does dance present an opportunity to move beyond mind-body dual-
ism?

Because this study is one of the first works about Uzbek expressive arts,
I did not want to assume that theoretical models used to interpret dance
in Western contexts would be appropriate. I chose to juxtapose the dancers' verbal narratives about their lives and careers, with an examination
of some of the dances they performed. I built a framework for understanding Uzbek dance by asking the artists themselves what they intended to
express through dance. In turn, I viewed the artists' verbal narratives of
their careers in light of a second, gestural "narrative," the dances they
created and performed. I drew on my own perceptions in learning to
move through the forms of Uzbek dance to add a third, cross-cultural
viewpoint.

Since I studied Uzbek dance from the perspective of dancers, I found
the work of agency and practice theorists such as Anthony Giddens
(1984), Pierre Bourdieu (1977), and Sherry Ortner (1996) helpful in exploring the constraints and opportunities dancers encountered in their
careers. I also used an approach grounded in practice theory to think
about whether and how dance and dancers embody, reproduce, and transform social order.

ORGANIZATION AND ANALYSIS

For purposes of discussion, I divided the seventy years covered by this study into four periods. As I began to look at the life histories in terms of cohorts and ages sets, patterns in the life histories began to emerge. Relationships among dancers tended to cluster into professional "generations" at intervals of fifteen to twenty years, the average working life of a dancer. Without prompting from me, dancers also identified themselves as members in a group of specific dancers who were their contemporaries. Each generation of dancers shaped institutions that created constraints and opportunities for the next generation of dancers. Furthermore, major trends in career and life paths for dancers roughly coincided with major historical events. Viewed within frames of lives and events, dances from different years became vivid records of contemporary concerns. Accordingly, I grouped the life histories and dances into four phases, which roughly coincide with significant historical events:

The October Revolution and The Early Soviet Years (1924–1942)

The first dance company was founded in 1929, and the first dancers were trained and recruited during these years.

World War II and The Postwar Period (circa 1943–1953)

During the late 1930s and 1940s, a second cohort of dancers chose dance as a career and began their training. World War II significantly changed the role of dancers in society as they joined the armed forces and went to the front to entertain the soldiers. Artists, scholars, and critics displaced by the war or by Stalin's policies founded theaters and institutes for studying the arts.

Industrialization and Development (circa 1954–1990)

Relationships between Uzbekistan and Moscow strengthened. Artists who began their careers after the postwar years trained in Moscow or worked with pan-Soviet companies. 1954 was also the beginning of the Khrushchev era.

Independence (1991–1994)

Dance was a prominent feature of the new cycle of national holidays and a medium for renegotiating collective identities. Some dancers and teachers left Uzbekistan to work abroad while others struggled with inflation at home.

Each chapter examines a different period from the years 1924 to 1994. I present life histories of women who began dancing in each of the four phases, and analyze dances from those periods. I examine the data from these two sources in light of a different aspect of modernization. Chapter 1 provides ethnographic data about gender, kinship idioms, and urban and rural family life as a foundation for exploring relationships among dance, gender, kinship, and nationalism. Chapter 2 discusses recruitment of the first Uzbek dancers and the role of the first dance companies as tools of nation building. Chapter 3 examines dance training as a ritual inculcating a sense of national identity in dancers. Chapter 4 studies dance as a cultural resource developed in a colonial empire. Chapter 5 explores how national dance was an arena of contest over disparate notions of Uzbek identity in the independent republic.

NOTES

1. For purposes of this study I have given real names of deceased individuals, authors of publications, and public figures. I also used the real names of some of the senior artists I interviewed, with their permission, because they would like their work to be known outside of Uzbekistan. I have followed the more conservative anthropological practice of using pseudonyms with younger performers and with nonperformers. Throughout the text, I have used full names (first name and surname) for real names. All single first names without surnames are pseudonyms. Although interview participants received only token gifts of appreciation, several mentioned to me that they encountered jealousy because people thought I had paid in dollars or provided substantial presents. I have also given no geographic locations of interviews or incidents relating to rural areas because the communities are too small for anonymity. I have tried to balance the competing goals of sharing the texture and warmth of our conversations with maintaining confidentiality. I apologize both to those who might remain recognizable and to those who would have enjoyed seeing their real names appear.

2. I thank an anonymous reviewer of this manuscript for helpful and provocative questions about gender, kinship idioms, and nationalism.

3. I am indebted to Stephan Miescher (1997) for coining the term "interview partner" as an alternative to the awkward word "informant."

4. Rodgers studied the written autobiographies of two men who grew up in colonial Indonesia. She found resonances between autobiographical and historical discourse based on the images and "scenarios" from Indonesia's rich oral and textual traditions. I am not relying on a similar literary analysis in this study of Central Asian women to explore the dialectic between individual and social history. Instead, I am tracing a parallel between changes in individual outlook and the context of social changes occurring during the Soviet and post-Soviet eras.

5. Bauman (1977: 17–18) notes that speakers often use figurative language as a keying device.

1

Gender, Kinship, and Nationalism

As I will discuss in the following chapters, national dances and dancers were initially part of a Soviet program directed at changing the indigenous Central Asian kinship structure by recruiting women as participants in Soviet programs. Dance was part of a broader program to bring women out of the home and into public life. The underlying issue of this study then concerns the interrelationships among gender, kinship idioms, dance, and nationalism. In order to understand the impact of national dances on the kinship structure and the lives of women and their families, it is helpful to understand the life cycle for women and dominant kinship idioms.

"A DAUGHTER IS A GUEST"

In the "traditional" indigenous Central Asian life cycle women progressed from a child, to a bride and servant to a mother-in-law, then to mother, finally becoming a mother-in-law and grandmother in her own right. Turning first to daughters, a popular Uzbek aphorism is "a daughter is a guest in her family's home." The saying reflects practices governing descent and marriage. Marriage is virilocal: Daughters are temporary members of kin groups, who leave upon marriage and join their husband's families. A girl's dowry consists of a large wardrobe, and all of the furnishings for a new home, including furniture, dishes, and linens. Thus, like guests, daughters require considerable expenditures and eventually leave. Another saying is that a man with seven daughters is guaranteed a place in Paradise. Daughters require dowries, so the burden of raising and arranging a marriage for a girl is heavy.

Sons, on the other hand, are prized. One of the first questions women discuss when meeting is about children. Women would smile fondly when saying they had daughters, but beam with pride if they had sons.

MARRIAGE AND MOTHERS-IN-LAW

Girls are marriageable at sixteen and begin to adopt very demure behavior. Although young girls dance with skill and panache, as soon as they reach sixteen their dancing at events such as weddings becomes restrained and subdued. One fourteen-year-old girl gleefully demonstrated Uzbek dance for me at home, incorporating many of the movements of professional dancers she had learned from television. Two years later I attended a cradle party where she stood with a group of other teenage girls, gently shuffling her feet and circling her wrists, as though she barely knew how to dance.

Kelins (brides) become members of their husband's family. The transformation is symbolized by the ritual of the bride's first visit to her natal family after her marriage. She can no longer sit at her family's table, but must crouch by their low table as she greets her family. Then she seats herself at the head of a separate table, joined by her friends and relatives. When she leaves, her natal family throws stones at her car as it pulls away, to say "do not come back."

The tension between mothers-in-law and brides is widely acknowledged. The open discussion of this issue was unusual; Uzbeks were generally reluctant to criticize others, at least in my hearing. A new bride is supposed to be her mother-in-law's servant. If the bride marries the youngest son, they will often live with his parents and inherit the family residence after caring for his parents during their old age. The house, however, is considered the bride's domain from the day of her marriage.

Conflicts between a mother and daughter-in-law were dramatized in popular culture. The Uzbek pop singer Yulduz Usmanova released a song criticizing mothers-in-law while I was in Uzbekistan in 1994. One line said: "A mother-in-law, how she boils you." I heard the song frequently on television and booming from kiosks on the streets, and was told that Usmanova had recently divorced. A television movie showed a middle-aged man driving with his mother to a field. Promising to return, he escorts her to a shady tree with a blanket. As she waits, she reminisces about how she had convinced her own husband to abandon his mother in a field. The day grows long and her son does not return. The old woman finally realizes that she has been abandoned, like her mother-in-law.

The instances I saw of relationships between brides and mothers-in-law were less dramatic than these two examples from the popular media. I had my first inkling of a bride's lot when I stayed overnight in a wealthy household. I awoke to the sound of splashing water at about two A.M. It was one of the brides in the household hunched over an outside irrigation ditch, doing laundry by hand.

Dancers told me that a mother-in-law was often a major barrier to performing after marriage. If a dancer continued to work after she married, the mother-in-law would be unhappy because her daughter-in-law would not be as available to help with the housework. One dancer bitterly cited her mother-in-law as the main cause of her recent divorce. Not all relationships, however, were difficult. One young woman told me that her mother-in-law cared for her son during the day, so that she could continue to work.

"PARADISE LIES AT A MOTHER'S FEET"

Brides usually had their first child within the first year or two of marriage. Since women began to marry at about age eighteen in Tashkent, this meant that the young women I saw were trying to please new in-laws, care for a newborn, and complete their studies. One institute teacher told me she saw female students with demanding mothers-in-law fall behind in their studies after marriage. Working mothers had the option of taking three years of maternity leave per child or placing their children in a *boghcha*, or children's garden, a form of free state-run day care.

Motherhood was perhaps the most important role in a woman's life. Men and women were greatly troubled by the fact that I was in my thirties, single, and childless. "Who will care for you when you are old?" they asked with concern. As I attended more weddings, cradle parties, and other family gatherings, I realized that children are a woman's path to influence in her husband's family.

A *kelin* leaves her natal home and enters her husband's household as her mother-in-law's servant. Bearing and raising children, and successfully arranging marriages for them, are the means through which a solitary, powerless *kelin* acquires status and authority within her husband's family. Her children, daughters-in-law, and grandchildren become her base of support within her husband's kin group. Women give birth to their own empires.

Although both fathers and mothers are openly affectionate toward their children, the bond between mother and child carries deep sentimental import. Even mentioning the tie evoked an instant and overwhelming emotional response. In conversation, women separated from their mothers by death or geographic distance became tearful when mentioning their mothers; men would look down and become silent and downcast for a long moment. Men and women often offered me sympathy because I was so far from my mother while I lived in Uzbekistan. Separation from fathers or other family members was also a great hardship, but people seemed more accepting of these dislocations as difficulties in the normal course of work, education, or marriage.

HUSBANDS AND WIVES: SEPARATE BUT EQUAL?

Conflicts I observed between husbands and wives clarified the responsibilities of each. One acquaintance received recognition for something she had accomplished professionally, at a time when her husband's work was meeting with many snags. He derided her achievement, asking her if it would bring in a substantial sum of money. To appease him, she made a meal requiring several hours of intensive labor. Her olive branch was accepted when he ate the meal in grudging silence, and peace was restored.

As for a husband's duties, I was surprised one day when I visited a new acquaintance. Her husband seemed quite deferential. In a reversal of the usual division of labor, he brought us a pot of tea, and politely requested her to slice him a plate of onions, instead of the customary blunt demand for food. She confided that he had been unfaithful, but the affair was over. She told him that if he wanted to come back, he had better start earning a lot more money, as their children were reaching marriageable age.

These episodes highlight the basic responsibilities of spouses. Men bring home money, while women prepare food and serve guests. Reversal of these roles led to tension, in the instance of the working woman, whose success infringed upon her husband's role as primary breadwinner. In the second instance, an erring husband took on some domestic responsibilities to appease his angry wife, in addition to increasing his efforts to add to the family coffer.

The ways these two couples resolved their tensions further reflects a hierarchy between husbands and wives. The successful wife had to please her husband by making an extra effort in the kitchen. The straying husband had to express his contrition by taking on the traditionally female task of helping to make tea and serve a guest. In both instances, performing domestic duties associated with the wife's role was a means of assuming a subservient position.

OLD AGE

Men and women acquired more status with age. Their children and grandchildren deferred to their wishes and contributed to their care. As mentioned above, youngest sons would care for their parents in their old age and inherit the natal residence. I also observed that even when the youngest child was a daughter rather than a son, the relationship between the youngest child and the parents was especially warm and loving.

I noticed few elderly men at events such as weddings but many white-haired women. People said men in Uzbekistan had a much lower life expectancy rate than women, because men smoked and drank.[1] At many social events such as weddings bottles of vodka and cognac sat in the center of the table along with bottles of *gazli su* (carbonated water), *li-monad* (soda pop), and Coca Cola. Men poured rounds of vodka into their teacups. In Tashkent, women would occasionally accept a teacup of vodka or cognac. By the end of the evening, young men were often quite bois-terous and red-faced, stomping explosively on the dance floor. In rural areas, I do not recall seeing women drink at all, although men drank both during tea and at weddings.

The importance of seniority combined with the lower life expectancy of men gave mature women considerable power and authority as they aged. For instance, one grandmother declared in late spring that her grandson must marry, and the search for a suitable bride began. I at-tended the wedding held less than three months later.

COLONIALISM AND FEMINISM

The Soviets introduced many reforms to bring women into public life. Instead of keeping *purdah* and staying at home, women entered profes-sions, especially medicine and teaching. Day care was readily available in government-run *boghchalar.* Although these and many other measures seemed to resemble desirable reforms the American feminist movements applauded during the 1970s, there was a certain irony. Where feminism in the United States had been a movement led by women, for women, the changes to women's lives in Uzbekistan had occurred under the aegis of a colonial government. In a certain sense, the Soviet State had forced Muslim women in Uzbekistan to be "liberated."

I was not sure what bearing this difference would have on understand-ing the impact of the Soviet period on gender, but I began to suspect that it was very significant. While a more complete exploration of this question will require further study, my preliminary impressions suggested that com-paring lives of rural and urban women is likely to be fruitful. Women I met in rural areas led more "traditional" lives in the sense that they had limited education and devoted themselves to caring for their large fami-lies. On the other hand, I met women in urban areas who had participated in Soviet programs for women. They were educated, with one or two chil-dren, and many had or aspired to successful careers.

I stayed with two families, one rural and one urban, for short visits. I will describe daily life to illustrate how the indigenous life cycle for women is similar for both rural and urban women.

Women in urban areas such as Tashkent were more affected by Soviet programs than rural women, as illustrated below in the comparison of Mariamkhon's and Nodira's daily routines. The daily life I saw was also affected by my presence as a guest, requiring more attention to food and showing me the house and neighborhood.

I visited a rural household in an agricultural region of Uzbekistan. The family consisted of a grandmother, her son, his wife, and a grandson who was about two years old. Early in the morning, the family huddled in a chilly room around a low table, slurping hot milk with tea with chunks of buttered bread floating in the milk. The young wife, Nodira, did not sit with us, but moved back and forth between the kitchen and the table, serving everyone and bringing fresh pots of tea. Several other men also sat at the table; one was the husband's brother. When the meal was over, the men left and I did not see them again until after dark.

The husband in the family was the youngest son; he and his wife Nodira would inherit the *howli* (family compound) when his mother died. Nodira worked constantly while I was there, cleaning, cooking, baking, and feeding the household animals. She worked with steady rhythm and sturdy cheer. I watched her doing dishes after lunch using water from the outside pump. Her hands were red and chapped. She scrubbed the plates with an energetic, circular motion, then the large *qozon*, a steel pot like a wok. I felt that she enjoyed showing me her skills as a housewife, and her cleaning became a kind of dance. Her circular sweeps continued, scooping water out of the *qozon*. Without hurrying, the dishes were soon stacked on the boarded table by the pump, and she was ready to move on to her next task.

One day Nodira baked bread. She baked it in a clay oven called a *tandoor*. The *tandoor* was in a room with no door and was a hollow mound with an opening high on one side. It looked like a small cave. Nodira started a fire in the *tandoor* and added sticks. She let the wood burn down to white coals. When the dough was ready, she formed it into large flat rounds about the size of a medium pizza. She poked holes in them using a device made of wood with embedded thin metal spikes. Reaching into the oven through the opening, she slapped the dough onto the heated sides of the oven and splashed them with water. The rounds were removed with the help of scorched, tattered mitts and a large spatula. *Non* (bread) is a staple at every meal. *Tandoor non* is considered the best bread. In cities, apartment dwellers have only gas ovens and no *tandoors*, so rural families bake and sell *tandoor non* on streets and outside subway stops throughout Tashkent.

Bread is a dietary staple, and an important symbol as well. Learning to make bread is an important step in a woman's life. While the bread dough was rising, I asked how to tell when the dough was ready. Looking at me out of the corner of her eye, as though imparting a great secret, the grandmother pulled the dough with her forefinger and pointed to tiny black airholes pocking the dough. I wondered why the women had seemed so dramatic in telling me how to test bread dough. Later I learned that a woman learned to bake bread from her mother-in-law. As a single woman, I was not supposed to know how to make bread yet.

One afternoon after lunch I wrote notes and sipped tea, sitting outside with the grandmother and the grandson. We sat on an open platform called an *aywon*, a space about ten feet by ten feet, covered by a tablecloth. In warm weather, families dine together outside on the *aywon*, and it is one of the vital centers of the home. While the young mother worked caring for the house, the grandmother watched the toddler. "What are you writing?" the grandmother asked me. I told her I was writing about the *howli*, and how they grow vegetables and make honey. She looked pleased when I stopped writing. Noting her satisfied smile, thereafter I cut my note-taking sessions short, albeit reluctantly.

The grandmother took me on a tour of the compound. The house was built in a rectangle around a large open courtyard. Much of the space was devoted to a garden, with peach trees, pomegranate bushes, carrots, onions, and peppers. The family also owned goats and a cow. Honey came from a bee box. The grandmother plucked two full, perfect roses and presented them to me with a gracious nod.

We went on a walk to a nearby field where children played. The grand-mother led the toddler by the hand. They looked oddly alike, progressing over the yellow, dried grass with halting, rocking steps. They seemed like boon companions and were virtually inseparable. The field was apparently part of the neighborhood school. I wanted to take pictures of the children playing, but as soon as I pulled out my camera, the children raced from all ends of the field and posed for a photograph in a cluster in front of me.

Another day included a visit for tea at the husband's brother's house. My hostess changed from her sweater, kerchief, and faded housedress to a bright, sheer scarf on her head and a colorful *atlas* (silk ikat fabric) dress with leggings. Her cheerful, tanned sister-in-law had four children although she was only twenty-four. When we returned, I commented that she was young to have so many children. To my surprise and dismay, Nodira's eyes filled with tears. I realized that even though she was only twenty, she was terribly upset that she had only one child so far, while her sister-in-law already had a large family.

In the rural household I visited, men's and women's lives were clearly segregated. Women stayed home and raised children, cleaned house, cooked, and tended livestock. Men were gone most of the day working outside the home. When there were men at home, the wife waited on them, bringing them tea and food. The baby sat at the table for meals, and the grandmother and father shared his care.

In the urban household where I lived while looking for permanent housing, the couple had only one child—a daughter. She had married a young man in the neighborhood and had one child. The young couple lived with the husband's parents in a compound nearby. All were members of the intelligentsia.

The day began with breakfast, usually hot tea, with soup and bread left over from the night before. I set the table while Mariamkhon heated the food. Tursin joined us at the table for his meal, then left for work. Mariamkhon and I did the dishes and she left for work around ten. I left at the same time either searching for a permanent place to live or making research contacts.

Mariamkhon and I returned about three to start dinner. She changed out of her work clothes (a stylish black skirt and sweater) into a worn printed housedress and slippers. She told me to make the table *chiroyli* (pretty), which meant cleaning crumbs off the tablecloth and setting out teacups and spoons. While I set the table, she began dinner: a *shorba* made of carrots, onions, potatoes, tomatoes, and lamb with cumin and salt. I helped peel potatoes and chop vegetables. While we cooked, she would talk to me about Uzbek culture—history, family life, or religion. Once dinner was simmering on the stove, Mariamkhon would say her prayers. With independence, Islamic observance was becoming more popular. Mariamkhon said with some pride that with independence, religion was again permitted, so that being a practicing Muslim was part of their pride in being an independent republic.

Tursin returned at dusk, often carrying a bag of fruit or vegetables from the market. Shopping was his responsibility. Mariamkhon served tea and dinner, and we ate together while Mariamkhon and Tursin chatted. Afterward, I did the dishes. Mariamkhon usually scolded me for making too much noise and clanking the dishes. Sponges were one of the many items that became unavailable when Uzbekistan declared independence from the Soviet Union, so I did the best I could with the worn scrap that was all Mariamkhon had left of her sponge. The evening ended with everyone watching a Russian detective movie, which was Tursin's favorite type of program.

Mariamkhon told me about the *qöshni qöshnisin bazari* (the neighbor's bazaar). When one neighbor went to the market, she would knock on a neighbor's door to see if she needed anything. Mariamkhon offered to take out her neighbor's trash when she took her own out to the dumpster about a block from her apartment. Neighbors also brought by a plate of food when they cooked something special.

When I found my own apartment, my neighbors were very sympathetic. The teenage daughter of the house took me to the neighborhood market, an open farmer's market, and showed me how to tell whether meat was fresh. I was also surprised one day to open the door and find two middle-aged women I had never met. They seemed equally surprised to see me. I asked friends who they might have been and was told that they were probably neighborhood matchmakers who had heard that there was an unmarried woman in the apartment.

Comparing the lives of rural and urban women in terms of the normative life cycle for women, the rural women I met led lives shaped by the traditional life cycle of marriage, motherhood, and eventually, for the fortunate, revered head of an extended family comprised of children, their spouses, and grandchildren. Some of the women I met had professional credentials; for instance, I met a language teacher and a young teenage bride who had graduated from medical school. They were home during the day when I visited and told me that the state provided three years of maternity leave for each child.

The rural women prided themselves on heading large clans of sons, daughters, and grandchildren. They seemed to be content and confident. By the time the women reached middle age, sons and daughters heeded their advice, brought them gifts, and tended to their needs. For those with children, particularly sons, seniority brought the happy prospect of greater authority and a loving community of children and grandchildren.

For urban women, too, marriage and motherhood were critical. Urban women tended to marry a few years later than rural women, but also had at least one child as soon as possible after marriage. Most had one or two children. Unmarried women of twenty-four or twenty-five expressed great anxiety about being nearly too old for marriage. The few women over thirty who had never married were anomalies. As a group, urban women I met seemed less content and often downright harried as they juggled the demands of children, spouses, employers, and relatives. Although quite proud of their professional achievements, at home these women were often quite deferential to their husbands, doing all the housework, cooking their favorite dishes, and agreeing with their opinions. Children, male and female, assisted their mothers with household tasks, but husbands rarely did, at least not in my presence.

As children married and established their own families, urban mothers lost the assistance provided by their children. A prospective bride's family generally expected the groom's parents to provide a separate apartment for newlyweds. I know of three families who lived in *howlis* who gained help because they could provide rooms in the compound for their son and new daughter-in-law, but parents who lived in apartments usually lacked enough space and had to provide a separate apartment for their son and his bride. Age and seniority thus often brought greater domestic burdens rather than help to urban women.

Rural women I met frequently expressed pity about urban women, with their small families. Urban men and women in turn shook their heads over the plight of rural women. Rural women lived in terrible conditions of poverty, lacked medical care, and had too many children. When I mentioned how content I thought rural women seemed to be, one urban

acquaintance said I was absolutely wrong. How could I possibly think that
those unfortunate rural women were happier than urban women?

KINSHIP: BLOOD AND MARRIAGE

Kinship ties in Uzbekistan remained, despite Soviet efforts, a resilient
and powerful basis for accomplishing social business. I made a rough
count of guests at weddings I attended by counting the number of tables
and the number of seats at the tables. The number usually came to about
300 people. Uzbeks tend to favor large families, so the extended family
saw each other frequently for life-cycle celebrations, such as marriages and
cradle parties for newborns. Friends who invited me greeted many people
by name, and almost always knew the identity of anyone if I asked. The
bride's and groom's families celebrate at separate feasts on two different
evenings, so the tally of 300 only represents celebrants from one side of
the marriage.

Kinship structure followed a pattern familiar in many Muslim and Central Asian societies (Bacon [1966] 1980: 68; Esposito [1988] 1991: 94).
Descent was determined patrilaterally. The primary family unit consisted
of parents, sons, and unmarried daughters, with variations described below. Marriage was virilocal, so that daughters left the natal home.

Residence and inheritance for married sons tended to follow a pattern
dating back to Genghis Khan. Genghis Khan divided his empire among
his four sons, leaving the family patrimony to his youngest son as "guard-
ian of the hearth" (Grousset [1970] 1996: 253–256). Similarly, in Uzbekistan the youngest son inherited the family compound and was responsible
for caring for his parents in their old age. He and his bride and children
lived with the parents. Elder sons established their own households upon
marriage or as soon after as possible.

I observed two kinds of primary family units, one following the indigenous Central Asian model, and a second resembling a Western nuclear
family. In rural areas, and in urban families occupying *howlis*, the primary
family unit followed a Central Asian model and consisted of parents and
unmarried children of both sexes. The youngest son and his spouse and
children also lived with the family, but older married sons generally had
their own residences or planned to as soon as financially possible.

One urban family in Tashkent, for example, occupied a *howli* with two
courtyards. The first courtyard and surrounding rooms belonged to one
brother, and the other was occupied by a second brother and his family.
The first courtyard had belonged to the brothers' parents, who were deceased. The second brother and his wife had three sons. They built two
units in his half of the compound in anticipation of the day the boys would
marry. The groom's family had to provide housing upon marriage, and
the bride's family had to provide furnishings for her house and an elab-

orate wardrobe. In this family, the second brother and his wife were pleased because they had housing ready for two of their sons. The units, consisting of a kitchen, living room, and bedroom, would go to the eldest and youngest sons. The middle son would receive his own home outside the *howli* when he married.

I observed a different pattern of residence among families living in apartments. Tashkent has many high-rise apartment buildings. Most of the apartments I saw had a kitchen, a living room, a dining area, two bed-rooms, and a bathroom. The apartments were usually occupied by a nu-clear family of parents and unmarried children. A mother with one son said that sharing an apartment with her son and his bride would not be a good situation. Finding the money to buy an apartment for him was one of her major worries.[2] Apartment dwelling thus appeared to necessi-tate earlier fission of married sons and their families, even the youngest or only son. Although further studies would be necessary, it appears that Soviet colonization and modernization reduced the primary family unit for many urban families to a "Western" nuclear model.

MARRIAGE

Marriage was the second most important way of defining kinship. In many Muslim societies, the preferred partner for marriage is a parallel cousin, such as father's brother's daughter. Scholars such as Pierre Bour-dieu ([1977] 1995: 30–58) found that the normative preference for par-allel cousin marriage, however, did not govern actual marriage practices.

I found many instances in which a bride was marrying a "relative" (*gar-indosh*). *Garindosh* was a broad term usually used for someone who was not a person's grandparent, parent, sibling, spouse, or child. As oppor-tunity permitted I tried to obtain more specific information about the kinship ties between a bride and groom. I could not verify any instances in which parallel cousins married.

I began taking field notes to see whether Uzbek marriage practices re-flected a preference for parallel cousins, but realized after about seven months that people had used the term *aka* (elder brother) to refer to a wide variety of male relatives. The term could mean ego's older brother but was also a respectful and affectionate term for male relatives older than ego, such as an uncle on the mother's or the father's side, a cousin, a brother-in-law, or even a brother of a brother-in-law. Similar ambiguity applied to *uka* (younger brother) and *opa* (elder sister). As a result the data I gathered about endogamy in rural areas was inconclusive.

My data suggest dramatic differences in marriage practices between ur-ban and rural couples. Although I did not ask everyone I met, I found no cases in which women from Tashkent married relatives. All had married coworkers or classmates from school. My data on marriages outside of

Tashkent is limited, but most women said their husbands were "relatives." In one village, an adolescent girl said everyone in the village was related.

Normatively, people expressed a preference for marrying relatives. One friend was considering an offer from a young man related to her mother's family. Although she did not particularly care for him, she was considering his suit seriously because she knew that the in-laws would get along. I asked a woman who had married a classmate from her institute why people said they preferred to marry relatives but did not. She said, "Our families prefer to give us to relatives, but we do not prefer it."

People told me that Uzbek women had to marry Uzbek men. Uzbek men could and frequently did marry women of Russian or Tatar descent. However, I know of three instances in which an Uzbek woman married a non-Uzbek: One married a European, a second married an American, and a third met and married a Russian man in Moscow. I suspect that the prohibitions on exogamy are based on Muslim law which permits men to practice exogamy, provided they marry "people of the book," that is to say Christians and Jews. Muslim women, however, must marry Muslim men. Despite seventy years of atheist rule, Uzbeks still observed these asymmetrical practices governing exogamy.

KINSHIP AS A PARADIGM FOR NATIONAL UNITY

Despite the fragmentation of households I observed among urban areas, cooperation among households, especially among adult siblings, remained strong. The family unit also appeared to be an important paradigm for political organization. *Kon* (blood) was a powerful tie, sustained despite geographic separation. Cynthia Werner's fruitful research (1997) on intra-household cooperation in Kazakstan indicates that intra-household cooperation in Uzbekistan is likely to be a rich area for future study. My data suggest that relationships between siblings and relatives by marriage are most important. Neighbors are also occasional sources of goods and assistance.

The bond among brothers is important both normatively and in practice. A popular Central Asian proverb tells of a father on his deathbed who calls together his four sons. He hands each a single stick and tells them to break their stick. The sticks snap easily. He offers a bundle of four sticks and asks each son to break it. None can. The motto of the story is that individually the brothers are weak; but united, they could not be defeated. The first man who told me the story was a member of the intelligentsia who attributed the story to Genghis Khan and his four sons.

The ideal of cooperation among siblings was evident in many aspects of Uzbek life. One family of brothers I met lived next to each other in adjacent *howlis*. Siblings also contributed labor to each other's households. Tursin worked many Saturdays in the garden of his natal *howli*. Later in the year, he received a share of the fruits and vegetables the garden produced. Sisters frequently helped each other with cooking and entertaining guests. Solidarity also prevailed among brothers and sisters. For instance, as discussed further in Chapter 5, a sister could help a brother find a bride.

Households also cooperated across urban and rural lines. I know of at least two families in which educational opportunities during the Soviet period resulted in patterns in which some siblings remained in a rural area, while another sibling moved to an urban area for school and secured employment in a city after graduation. Visits from city to country were opportunities for exchange of goods available in each area. Urban relatives sometimes provided housing to daughters of rural relatives while the young women studied at institutes in the city. Weddings and cradle parties were occasions of redistribution.

I attended one wedding where the bride's mother's sisters contributed items costing about a month's salary to the bride's dowry. People told me that the nice people in Uzbekistan were usually not the wealthy people. They could only become rich by refusing to share with their families and relatives.

ADOPTION

A third idiom of kinship that plays an important part in nationalist discourse is adoption. As I discuss further in Chapter 5, adoption is a metaphor for uniting the diverse peoples of the Soviet Union as siblings. In downtown Tashkent, a monument known as *Halqlar Dostligi* (People's Friendship) honors a blacksmith and his wife who adopted children from each of the Soviet republics during World War II.

Adoption is a powerful metaphor for nationalist discourse because it resonates on many levels. It appeals to the Uzbek pride in generosity and love of children. It is also consistent with *zakat*, the obligation of devout Muslims to provide for the poor. Cooperation among siblings, as exemplified by the parable of the brothers and the sticks, is an ideal in Uzbekistan. In practice, siblings and parents comprise the fundamental family unit in kinship structure. Siblings assist each other in gathering resources to marry children, obtaining scarce goods and undertaking large tasks such as planting gardens and cooking feasts for guests.

Although I was a foreigner and the first American most Uzbeks had met, adoption was an idiom mature married women often used to define our relationship. Women with adult children referred to me as *qizim* (my daughter) if our relationship developed from a formal relationship of guest and host into a more comfortable and friendly level. One dance teacher who called me *qizim* cooked a meal for me after every class and brewed a tonic for me when she thought I was anemic. A rural grandmother poked my nonexistent bicep and joked that she would find me a local husband. Would I be strong enough to slap *non* onto the sides of a *tandoor* to bake it?

Whereas a bride or groom had to be carefully selected and occupied a strictly defined place in a household marriage, adoption was a flexible and inclusive device for incorporating people from unfamiliar kin groups and ethnicities. If anything, the more far-flung the connection, the greater the generosity of the adoptive "parent." Adoption was thus a kind of extended hospitality, a way to account for guests who stayed beyond a few days, or for whom one wished to express affection.

WOMAN OR GIRL? GENDER AND FIELDWORK

Having come of age in the United States during the 1970s, I had shaped my own life in terms of the new opportunities and ideologies of middle-class feminism. I graduated from Yale College in 1977, the second class of women to attend the college for all four years. Determined to have a career which would afford me independence, I chose to become an attorney and graduated from Harvard Law School in 1980. My class was about 30 percent women, and a cohort became part of the first wave of women to enter the legal profession in large numbers.

Regardless of whatever people in urban areas of Uzbekistan said about supporting notions such as education, careers, and health care for women, I found that, in practice, I had much to understand. Precepts such as equality, self-reliance, assertiveness, and initiative that I had long accepted as norms, if not realities, of my life as a career woman were quickly cast into oblivion when I arrived in Uzbekistan. As an unmarried woman, I was a "girl," with the same social status as a child.

Being a "girl" meant that I had virtually no authority in a situation. I was supposed to be quiet and self-effacing. As a guest, however, I could ask for assistance. The best way to cope with issues from managing official red tape to finding a driver was not to step up and handle the matter myself, as an American attorney would. Instead, the quickest and smoothest solution was to quietly and privately make requests as a guest to friends or acquaintances, who usually could find someone through their extended kinship networks who could resolve the problem.

As I looked for long-term housing, Mariamkhon and her husband were very protective of me and concerned for my safety. I left the house about ten in the morning when Mariamkhon left for work. I was expected to return by two-thirty or three when Mariamkhon returned. My daily rounds thus followed the same pattern as when I was in grade school, except that I was allowed to handle a sharp knife at Mariamkhon's to cut vegetables.

During my first two months in Uzbekistan, I chafed at the restrictions I had to live within as a single foreign woman. I resented being treated like a child again, and my initial reaction, as someone who had lived and participated in the women's movement in the United States, was outrage. As an anthropologist, I had to stifle my reactions and try to live with the sharp edge of "cultural relativism." I had come to Uzbekistan resolved to be as open-minded as I could. I had to get used to the fact that being an anthropologist was no protection against being judged by the people I had come to study. By their lights, I was a just a Japanese girl and a guest.

When Mariamkhon introduced me to her relatives, my father's profession, my access to scarce goods such as computers, and my status as a foreigner were the most important things about me. Although she knew about my educational background and credentials as an attorney, these were of no particular relevance. As a member of the intelligentsia and a working woman, Mariamkhon understood who and what I was better than many people I encountered.

Many people who eventually learned simply gave me blank stares or troubled looks when they learned I was unmarried and thirty-six. They asked whether I wanted children. Education and occupation could not explain or make up for the absence of husband and children in my life. At one feast a young woman sneered at me loudly and repeatedly because I was single. I finally became exasperated and fancifully told her that six men were asking my parents for my hand, and that two of them were very wealthy. Her disdain turned immediately to wide-eyed respect, and she began asking me if I would help her go to America.

I found temporary respite with other foreigners—graduate students spending the year in Uzbekistan. When we gathered for an occasional dinner or to celebrate an American holiday, I suddenly felt visible; I felt that I had a voice that others heard. And yet, when I saw Uzbek women in the street or in their offices and dance studios, they were hardly shy or fragile women. Although I felt undercut by the social system in which I found myself, these women must have had other bases of power and authority that were simply not yet visible to me.

CONCLUSION

The importance of kinship, marriage, motherhood, and seniority for women, which seemed initially so oppressive to me in my own encounters with Uzbeks, did not seem to be uniformly oppressive to Uzbek women. Domesticity certainly brought heavy demands to younger women, but also offered gains in status that increased over time. A young bride is supposed to be her mother-in-law's servant. Most brides also had their first child within the first or second year of marriage.

Sherry Ortner suggested reexamining issues of agency and actors in terms of the metaphor of a "serious game." She said:

The idea of the "game" is meant to capture simultaneously the following dimensions: that social life is culturally organized and constructed, in terms of defining categories of actors, rules and goals of the games, and so forth; that social life is precisely social, consisting of webs of relationship and interaction between multiple, shiftingly interrelated subject positions, none of which can be extracted as autonomous "agents" and yet at the same time there is "agency," that is, actors play with skill, intention, wit, knowledge and intelligence. The idea that the game is "serious" is meant to add into the equation the idea that power and inequality pervade the games of life in multiple ways, and that, while there may be playfulness and pleasure in the process, the stakes of these games are often very high. (1996: 12)

In the domain of the home, Uzbek women's lives progressed through a series of stages and challenges. The "traditional" path for an Uzbek woman was to marry, have a large family, accumulate capital for dowries and bride prices, and successfully marry off her children. Young girls and new brides had virtually no power and authority, but women acquired both as they progressed through the life cycle. Like a checker reaching the far row, a woman who maximized her opportunities and survived the pitfalls of a scheming mother-in-law, infertility, infidelity, divorce, and financial instability attained the position of mother-in-law and grandmother and became a *begim* (queen) of her own empire. Victorious players reaped the rewards of influence, respect, affection, and financial security.

The "game" of the life cycle for women provided a normative framework that women and their families tried to follow. In practice, however, the game was complicated by luck and by burdens and opportunities created by a Soviet program directed at women. Although the Soviets had encouraged women to enter the workforce since the 1930s, my experiences in the field quickly showed me the importance of thinking cross-culturally in terms of "feminisms."

NOTES

1. Barbara Anderson and Brian Silver (1990: 201) said that reported life expectancy at birth in 1958–1959 in the USSR as a whole, according to Soviet publications, was 71.7 for women and 64.4 for men. Noting that mortality data on Central Asia are problematic, Anderson and Silver (1990: 210–212) found that the life expectancy at birth in 1969–1970 was 74.6 years for Uzbek women and 68.5 years for Uzbek men.

2. "Buying" an apartment may be a new practice begun after independence. A Tashkent resident told me that apartments were provided by the state during the Soviet period. After independence, people owned their apartments privately and could buy and sell them. While the practice of providing housing to a son upon his marriage appeared to be well established in 1992 and 1994, the means of procuring housing may have changed. I did not realize the possible ambiguities

in meanings of the phrase "buy an apartment" until after I left Uzbekistan, and thus I did not gather data about it. A question beyond the scope of this study would be the nature and effect of privatization of home ownership on residence, inheritance, and marriage.

2

Taboo Breakers: The Early Soviet Years (1924–1942)

A brief background of pertinent social and historical developments sets the stage for discussing the lives and careers of three early national dancers. Muslim Central Asia fell under Russian rule during the second half of the nineteenth century. Prior to Russian conquest, the region consisted of emirates strategically located in southern oases and shifting confederations of pastoral nomads roaming the northern steppes. In 1924 the Soviets carved Muslim Central Asia into five republics: Uzbekistan, Kazakstan, Turkmenistan, Kyrghyzstan, and Tajikistan. In order to inhibit the possibility of resistance, the Soviets designated the borders to divide major ethnic groups so that each republic contained a majority of one ethnic group, and a minority of several other ethnic groups.

The borders of the SSR of Uzbekistan encompassed a majority of Turkic-speaking groups, and a minority of Tajik (Persian)-speaking ethnic groups. Although "Uzbek" was not the most historically appropriate ethnonym for the populace of the new republic, the Soviets selected the name "Uzbekistan" after much debate (Bauldauf 1991) since the population of the new republic included many ethnic groups. The gerrymandered borders in former Muslim Central Asia presented the Soviets with the problem of creating an Uzbek identity among historically disparate groups (1991).

The Soviets identified indigenous extended kinship structures as a critical basis of resistance to creating an "Uzbek" consciousness. Programs to change the roles of women became keys to reshaping family relationships. The formation of "national" dance companies served the needs of creating symbols of the new Uzbek republic, and of encouraging women to undertake roles in the public sphere.

LIFE BEFORE THE SOVIET PERIOD

Before discussing the lives of the first Uzbek dancers, a brief interview I conducted with Firuza, an elderly woman in a remote rural area, will give us a glimpse into life at the beginning of the Soviet period. Firuza said she was seventy-four, so she was born in 1920, the year the Russians subdued the last two independent Central Asian emirates, Khiva and Bukhara. I sat on a cushion on the floor with her female relatives: a daughter-in-law, granddaughter-in-law, and a neighbor related to the family.

I had already interviewed her daughter-in-law and her neighbor. I turned to Firuza and asked her to tell her story. To everyone's amusement the neighbor decided to take over the role of interviewer. I did not yet know the deferential grammatical forms I should have used, especially in speaking to women who were my elders. Listening to the tape of the interview, I now realize that the neighbor performed a good-humored parody of my rudeness in using a syntax that demanded instead of politely requested information.

Firuza was hard of hearing so her neighbor bellowed the questions in a piercing voice. Firuza mumbled through toothless gums. A white scarf wrapped her brown crinkled face. At times she broke into sobs remembering those she had outlived, became impatient with questions she deemed foolish or seemed to drift away from us looking at something only she could see and muttering.

Neighbor: That [pointing to the tape recorder] can write what you say.

Firuza: That—that can write what I say? Really?
(Everyone laughs)

Relative: She says tell about where you were born, your father and your mother.

Firuza: I am the daughter of Samarkhon. I am the granddaughter of Kalandar. I am the granddaughter of (unintelligible). They are all from here. They are all dead.

Relative: What is your age? How old was your mother?

Firuza: I am seventy-four years old . . .

MD: When did you get married?

Neighbor: She is saying "Tell us about your youth, your married life and how you pass your days."

MD: How was your wedding? What happened?

Firuza: My youth was smashing. My grandparents and in-laws were alive. All of these people passed on to the other world. The good world. I am going to be there too.

Neighbor: Talk about your marriage. What kind of bride were you?
(Everyone laughs)

Firuza: At fourteen I went to my husband's house. . . .

MD: Fourteen.

Firuza: I don't know what kind of bride I was [meaning that she was nothing out of the ordinary]. Once I was a bride. I lived all my life. I am so old now. It was good once, my child.

Neighbor: What did you ride? A donkey? Did they put you on a horse?

Firuza: I have ridden a horse. I have ridden a donkey. So?

Neighbor: So you passed the river (on the horse on the way to her husband's house)
. . .

With prompting, Firuza described her arrival at her husband's house. The fire she mentioned was the practice of carrying a new bride around a fire before she entered her new home. A young Uzbek anthropologist explained that the practice dated from pre-Islamic times. The meaning of carrying or leading the bride around the fire was to purify her. Grooms sometimes circled the fire too. The Uzbek scholar also said that after circling the fire, the bride and groom would see who could step on the other's foot. Whoever managed to get a foot on top would rule the house.

Firuza: After being taken around the fire while I was on the horse I was set down at the house. Later when we got there my husband stepped on my foot.

Neighbor: You got married when the weather was bad?

Firuza: I was on the horse and it was raining. Water squished in my boots. The water came halfway up the horse, oh yo.

Neighbor: They crossed the big river.

Firuza: Shao shao shao [imitating the sound of the rain]. My clothing was all wet. A woman brought a fire bowl [a bowl filled with warm ashes] in front of me. They thought I was cold. They said "Don't go there, ehhhh come here!" It was getting wet. I had no sense.

Firuza evoked a vital picture of her life as a young girl, married shortly after puberty and surrounded by her relatives and in-laws. Her wedding included ancient customs that some Uzbeks told me dated back to the pre-Islamic times, perhaps remnants of Zoroastrian fire worship. Women told me that a bride was supposed to serve her in-laws. Her surprise at the care she received in her husband's house as a new bride probably reflects her low status in the household. Her reminiscences of rural life further reveal a fundamental unity of kinship, community, and home.

EARLY SOVIET REFORMS

Strong Muslim values and family structures were critical factors making resistance to Soviet hegemony particularly strong in Central Asia (see, e.g., Rywkin 1990). Gregory Massell (1974) says the Soviets decided to recruit women as a "surrogate proletariat" to lead the vanguard of reforms and to undermine the strong kinship networks. Propaganda decried practices such as polygamy, arranged marriages, and poor health care for women. New laws provided women with rights to suffrage, equal pay for equal work, and divorce. The Soviets exhorted women to leave their families and husbands for new freedoms provided by the Soviet system (1974). In 1919 the Soviet government began its vigorous campaign of recruiting women (1974). Women were urged to leave the home and were given opportunities to enter the workplace.

Massell notes that theatrical performance was one of the ways in which women were informed about Soviet programs and persuaded to participate (1974: 175n., 239–244). The first Uzbek national dance company was established in 1928, four years after the Soviets created the SSR of Uzbekistan, and instigated a massive program to transform Uzbek society through changing the lives of Uzbek women. An eminent Uzbek scholar recounted the evolution of national dance companies in Uzbekistan during the Soviet period in the following manner: Prior to the Soviet period women and boys danced in private settings. Boys and girls also danced in public settings, but not on the stage. In the pre-Soviet period, most professional dancers were boys who wore women's clothing.

A small group of individuals established Uzbek art and traditions in the twentieth century. One of these pioneers was Muhayiddin Kari Yakubov, a reciter of the Quran and a gifted singer. He created Uzbekistan's first troupe of dancers and musicians in 1928. He initiated the performance of dance, music, and singing together and brought Uzbek dance to the stage. One of the innovations that Kari Yakubov's new performing troupe instituted in 1928 was to put young girls on the stage.

The performing groups usually featured male musicians, male and female vocalists, and female dancers. A photograph (not shown) of Kari Yakubov's company taken at the first USSR International Olympiad in 1930 shows seventeen men and five women (Avdeyeva 1989: 70). Five of the men are holding instruments; one is holding a *doira* (a percussion instrument resembling a large tambourine) and four are holding long-necked stringed instruments. Avdeyeva identifies one of the women as Halima Nasirova, and two of the other women as Tamara Khonim and Mukarram Turghunbayeva, who were to become two of Uzbekistan's greatest dancers (1989: 70).

TAMARA KHONIM

Tamara Khonim was a well-known figure throughout Uzbekistan and the Soviet Union. She was the first woman in Uzbekistan to perform in public without a veil. Born Tamara Petrosian, she grew up in Uzbekistan but was of Armenian descent. Her stage name, Tamara Khonim, means literally Lady (*khonim*) Tamara. She died in 1991, the year before my first trip to Uzbekistan. I learned of her life and career history from Oydin, and Gulnara. Oydin was a retired dancer. Gulnara was the granddaughter of one of Tamara Khonim's musicians. Both women knew Tamara Khonim well and recalled her with great fondness.

Gulnara offered to show me the museum established in Tamara Khonim's former home in a bustling neighborhood in the center of Tashkent. In the short distance from the metro stop I walked down a wide four-lane avenue by the shiny plate glass store windows of a *gastronome*, a store selling delicacies such as sausage, soda, cookies, and cheese. Small kiosks like carnival booths overflowed with items from China, Iran, and America such as gum, chocolate, sweaters, batteries, pens, small plastic purses, instant coffee, and lipsticks.

Gulnara waited for me near a large teahouse. An open-air grill filled the air with stinging smoke and the crackling sizzle of *shashlik* (skewers of marinated lamb). A narrow asphalt road to one side of the restaurant opened onto a wide paved road and a cluster of white high-rise buildings. Gulnara walked up to a set of intricately carved wooden doors in one of the buildings. We entered a small, dimly lit foyer dominated by a life-size painting of a woman in a flowing green robe and black braids hanging from under a peaked golden headdress. She smiled flirtatiously over one shoulder, and her black eyes seemed to look at us yet slightly beyond us.

To the left, a glass door led to the museum. Late afternoon sunlight streamed through windows lining a long room with a warm golden wooden floor. Tall glass cases holding costumes lined the walls. As we wandered among the cases and fingered delicate stitching and handwork, Tamara Khonim's friends told me about her career. Tamara Khonim was born in Marghilon, a region in the Farghana Valley, in 1906. Even as a child, she showed great talent as a dancer and was frequently asked to dance at social events such as weddings. A group of touring musicians led by a musician named Kari Yakubov came to play at her school. When they saw Tamara Khonim dance, they invited her to perform that evening. Over her family's objections, she decided to become a dancer.

The museum displays began with costumes from major regions of Uzbekistan, including a velvet gown encrusted with golden stitching from Bukhara. Tamara Khonim performed unveiled, and the director said that she wanted to encourage other women to come out from behind the veil. She adapted the wide, enveloping robe (*paranji*) and had more fitted dresses following the lines of arms and torso made for her performances.

In between the cases of Uzbek costumes there was a display wall. On it were a tattered playbill from Tamara Khonim's first performance in Paris and yellowed photographs showing a young woman with dark flashing eyes and waist-length braids standing in a row of male musicians. A second

Portrait of Tamara Khonim displayed in the
Tamara Khonim Museum, Tashkent.

photograph featured the same woman in a sleek sleeveless evening gown
close to her husband, the musician Kari Yakubov. My companions proudly
pointed out the gold medal Tamara Khonim had won at a folk dance
festival in London in 1935. I asked whether Tamara Khonim had ever
talked about being one of the first women performers in Uzbekistan.
Oydin nodded solemnly, and talked about a performance in which someone in the audience had fired a gun at the stage.
  A photograph of Noor Khon, a solemn young woman with rounded
features and an embroidered cap, held a prominent place on another

Photograph of Noor Khon in the Tamara Khonim Museum, Tashkent.

wall of photographs. Noor Khon was stabbed to death in 1928 by her brother for performing with Yakubov's new dance and music troupe (see also Swift 1968: 181). This tragedy shows how incendiary public dance performances by women were in the opening decades of the Soviet program. Every dancer I asked recognized Noor Khon's name and knew her story. Her tragic end has become one of the chartering myths of professional dancers. Her fate highlights the complex interplay between the new state-sponsored performing groups and traditional Central Asian culture.

The museum tour continued with costumes gathered from all over the world. In every country she visited, Tamara Khonim had invited an artist to teach her a dance and song in exchange for teaching an Uzbek dance and song. She was both a dancer and a gifted singer, with a song reper-

Costume display in the Tamara Khonim Museum, Tashkent. Costume on left is an example of Bukharan *zardozlik* (gold embroidery).

toire in over eighty languages. Her dress collection included costumes from Japan, China, Germany, Spain, the Ukraine, Khorezm, and Arabia. Even a single overseas trip confers high status in Uzbekistan: Tamara Khonim's international costume collection constituted a stunning display of social capital.

Oydin explained that Tamara Khonim married twice, once to the musician Kari Yakubov and a second time to a handsome young composer. She had two daughters, one by each husband. The first child became a painter, and the second a scholar of literature.

We finished the tour in a private part of the museum where Tamara Khonim had lived. We sat at a long, glossy dining table, on chairs with delicately curved legs and admired a china cabinet displaying fine china from Japan. Wistful looks crossed the faces of my hostesses as they recalled many happy gatherings around this table. We went into an adjoining room and perched on a divan facing a low dressing table with a huge round mirror placed to catch the light from the windows. Tamara Khonim used to sit at the table and apply cosmetics from France and Europe. A faint smell of perfume seemed to hang in the air as the tour ended and Oydin pressed an old playbill into my hand as a souvenir of my visit.

ROZIYA KARIMOVA

After the dancer Noor Khon was killed, the Soviet state recruited fifteen young girls from orphanages to dance in her stead. Roziya Karimova was one of the original dancers in Kari Yakubov's company, and one of the orphans recruited to dance after Noor Khon was killed. Karimova's remarkable accomplishments include becoming a famous Uzbek national dancer and a noted teacher.

Our acquaintance began in 1992 when I interviewed her in Tashkent. For our first meeting and every meeting thereafter, she was splendidly attired. The day we met, she wore a dress made of metallic material. Her shiny dark brown hair was coiled in a tidy chignon at the nape of her neck. Gold earrings the size of silver dollars dangled from her earlobes. Powder, rouge, eye shadow, and red lipstick completed her ensemble.

The daughter of an Uzbek father and a Russian mother, Karimova was born about the time of the Soviet revolution. Her family kept records of births in a Quran. She did not know her exact birth date because when she was born, there was no one to write her name in the register. Her parents passed away when she was three, and she was placed in an orphanage in the Farghana Valley, where she received some initial dance training. Her older sister took her to another province in the valley. There she lived with a kind foster family and attended elementary school.

I was separated from my father and mother from this age [three]. Then I was given to the orphanage in X*** province. Having been prepared at the orphanage, then I came to Y*** province. My elder sister took me. There were just the two of us without our parents. My sister and I were in tears . . . After she took me to Y*** province, she gave me to [one or two other?] elementary schools. I studied there. I stayed with foster parents. I was the sixth child. They were very poor themselves but they were very good people. Then most foster families were rich, they all had cars and houses. They were po-o-o-r. I was the sixth child. It was very good. While I went to elementary school I stayed there. Then I graduated from the elementary school and went to a *teknikum* [technical school].

When the artist Kari Yakubov saw her dance in a concert at the *teknikum*, he arranged for Karimova and several other youngsters to go to Samarkand for dance training. In Samarkand, the dancer Tamara Khonim asked Karimova to dance in front of a male musician. Karimova was a devout Muslim and refused. She and a friend planned to run away rather than dance in front of men. Kari Yakubov learned of their escape plan and frightened the girls into staying in school.

So we went. When we went, there was a male person playing a *doira*. Tamara Khonim was there asking us to dance for other males. I told her "no, we're not

Roziya Karimova in 1992.

going to dance in the presence of men." I am a *hajji*[1] now. My [relative] went for
me. I am now also a very religious person and my [relative] has gone and done
hajj for me in my place.

My [relative] was . . . a very nice person. He did it for me. (choking with sadness)
God bless him.

We decided to run away and decided not to stay in school. At this point a close
friend who was with me in the orphanage, elementary, and middle school went
through the whole thing too. She was taken to Samarkand, then the capital of
Uzbekistan. Later they changed it to Tashkent.

Karimova and her friend stayed and learned to dance. Their training
included learning to play musical instruments, such as the drum (*doira*),
and to dance using 117 movements (*harakat*).

Karimova was an outstanding student and began teaching in the early
1930s. She joined one of Uzbekistan's musical theaters and sang operatic
roles such as *Carmen*. She also served in the war, receiving decorations for
her service. In the 1950s she was transferred to a theater in Tashkent
where she worked until retirement.

After retiring from the stage, Karimova became a noted teacher in a
choreographic school where children receive professional dance training.
In her personal life, her brothers selected a husband for her although she
preferred someone else. Karimova and her husband had one son. After

her husband passed away, Karimova married for a second time but eventually divorced. She lives with a relative, and visits her nephews and nieces regularly. One of her nieces danced with the *Bahor* (Spring) Ensemble but has since retired.

When I returned in 1994, I studied Uzbek dance with her for six months. We met in her home and practiced in her living room. Karimova arranged for some musicians to play the music so I could tape it for our lessons. Karimova's home became a haven for me. She insisted that I was a *mehmon* (guest) and was adamant that I accept her hospitality as a gift. When an Uzbek dance student completes her studies and begins working, however, gifts to a mentor are common practice. I hope that when I return to Uzbekistan, she may finally allow me to reciprocate. An excerpt from my field notes conveys the warm atmosphere of Karimova's home:

I sit in Roziya's living room as she and her [relative] fix lunch. She insists on feeding me, even though it is a strain on her budget, I am sure. Wallpaper with . . . flowers faded to sepia tones, a cabinet with a glass case, where mementos are lovingly displayed—goblets, a china cat, a little box of perfume and some Natural Wonder eye shadow [a small gift I gave her when we met in 1992].

A pure white tablecloth graces a four-legged wooden table—walnut colored, like all of the furniture. Three chairs, one rickety, surround the table. A huge carpet hangs on one wall—a knotted oriental in cream, white, teal, black, and khaki. A sofa and two chairs . . . now faded and covered with woven tapestries, neatly draped. . . . Cushions—squares decorated with delicate embroidery circles of white, blue, green, yellow.

My notes from that day also convey the mood and method of our classes together. It was my third class with her:

And my teacher sits on the sofa like a queen in a brown and yellow flowered housedress. A brown, yellow, pink, and cream scarf knotted around her head.

She says "And"—a beat late, my wrists come up—and she begins to sing. "Nai nai nai, nai nai nai nai na" as I move through the *holat* [basic positions of the arms]. She gently rocks her shoulders—a delicate spiral of the torso—in time to the music, cuing me.

"Don't move your hips, you don't need it," she says, wiggling her tushy. She demonstrates the correct form again—a slight push of the foot, extended to the side starts the motion, the body moves as a flat piece—all one. No wiggles. I try again and she says "Yes, but slight." She stands up and demonstrates again. "Tiny [*kichkina*]," I say. "Yes" she says. And I do the sequence again as she sings "Nai nai nai nai" in a quavery voice. I concentrate on tiny rocks to the music and getting my hands, feet and arms through the sequence. "Very good [*Ancha yakshi*]," she says with a satisfied grin.

My lesson that day introduced me to a powerful femininity implicit in nuances of the unfamiliar steps.

Today, the new movements she shows me highlight the mouth and eyes. She looks at me and bends her arms across her sternum [forearms horizontal], elbows bent, palms down, hands slightly cupped, thumbs in [against the palms]. Hands [and forearms] are about seven inches away from the sternum.

She slowly circles her hands one over the other [like winding yarn], then her wrists circle—one hand comes to rest under the right elbow, pinky of the right hand floats to the center of her chin, palm out, pointing up to her mouth. Her head flicks from side to side, like a Balinese dancer, just tiny little flicks. Her eyebrows arched, eyes alight, she is suddenly a beautiful, alluring woman. As my head moves, my body does too. "Just the head," she says with an arch look, "just the head." There is a prurient element in this dance, for the tiny flicks of the head make the movement playfully seductive rather than merely pretty.

Karimova gave me a thoughtful and thorough introduction to the fundamentals of Uzbek dance. She taught me three Uzbek national dances, one from each of the three major regions: Farghana, Bukhara, and Khorezm. From Karimova's careful exposition of differences in the three regional styles, I concluded that Uzbek dance during the early Soviet years reflected the construction of an Uzbek national identity from the three historically important and diverse areas during the early years of the Soviet regime.

My own study of Uzbek dances gave me an appreciation of the variations and the technical challenges of each style. Each kind of dance had its own movement vocabulary, music, and costumes.

Farghana dances were soft, light, and lyrical. The names of the steps were pastoral: leaning tree, waves of water, bird's neck, and bird's eye. The music was usually a sprightly waltz.[2]

The movements of Bukharan dances were more dense, with contained movements strongly connected to the earth. Unlike Farghana dance, motifs were seldom iconic. Instead the movements tended to display the dancer's body. Three dancers said that Bukharan dance originated in the court of the emir of Bukhara. One dancer said that because Bukharan dancers performed for the emir, the dancer wanted to say "Look at me!" and attract individual notice. When I asked whether movements in the Bukharan dances had a particular meaning, one teacher shrugged. Another teacher gave meanings to some, but not all, of the movements. Bukharan dance could also be the most overtly seductive, a quality I found disconcerting (see Chapter 3).

The Khorezm dance Karimova taught me was playful. I wore bells on my wrists and mimed picking apples, winding yarn, and holding a burning candle. As far as I know the dance held no particular narrative meaning connecting these images. Khorezmian dance was also rhythmically exacting. Sharp freezes alternating with shimmering movements created a counterpoint between the bells on my wrists and the asymmetrical rhythms that gave the dance a witty, whimsical quality. She also created a

Portrait of Mukarram Turghunbayeva in Farghana costume displayed in the Bahor Theater, Tashkent.

fragment of a fourth dance in the Uyghur style for me. (Uyghurs are Uzbek-speaking Muslims in China and are a minority ethnic group in Uzbekistan. The Uyghurs I have met look Asian, with epicanthic eyefolds like mine, so Karimova may have been typecasting me.)

Her sharp comments about how younger dancers and choreographers

An example of a Khorezm dance costume.

blurred distinctions among the regional styles alerted me to look for the homogenizing impact of centralized training and further changes in the construction of Uzbek identity discussed in Chapter 3.

Ballet masters [Uzbek]. If something was pretty, whatever movement might be pretty in Khorezm, they mixed it into a Farghana dance, or they mixed a movement in Farghana into Bukharan style dance. Doing that does not work. It [dance] will become poor. It will become a training exercise. In this way [dance] will become confused. Each style is rich on its own, for example, the costumes and the dances.

Dances must be graceful [jilwa]. They should not resemble athletic exercise. They cannot be busy all the time [habib aylar olmaydilar]. Stopping, they pause, making a pose like this—here is how those must be. They must be graceful. Ah, if they happen to be [like] physical exercise they will not work.

MUKARRAM TURGHUNBAYEVA

A discussion of the opening decades of Uzbek dance would be incomplete without Mukarram Turghunbayeva. Turghunbayeva's mother was a dutar[3] player. No one I asked seemed to know who her father was. In 1929 she joined the first Uzbek national dance company and worked with its founder Kari Yakubov. According to her biography published just before the fall of the Soviet Union (Avdeyeva 1989), she joined hobby groups in her normal school, including the song and dance ensemble. She told no one but her grandmother about her interest in theater and dancing.

It was from her that young Mukarram heard about mother, a talented singer, who had died young. The old woman also told her granddaughter about Mukarram, a dancer, in whose honour the girl had been named. Mukarram Turghunbayeva was too timid to make the final decision of joining the stage. Besides, she thought that artistes were extraordinary people while she held herself as a very ordinary person. (Avdeyeva 1989: 198)

Noor Khon's death, however, prompted Turghunbayeva to choose the theater. According to her biography, she ran away from home to join Kari Yakubov's company (1989: 198).

This brief biographical account raises as many questions about Turghunbayeva as it answers. I was repeatedly told that women did not dance in public before the Soviet period. Who then was "Mukarram," the dancer for whom Turghunbayeva was named? How did she know what "artistes" were like? If Turghunbayeva's mother died when she was young, who raised her? The information on her family is scanty. Most Uzbeks I met know at least 300 relatives by name, and see them regularly at life cycle events. Marriage is virilocal. Yet Turghunbayeva's biography gave no information about her father's family or any relatives other than her grandmother and mother.

The tour guide in Turghunbayeva's museum did not know anything about her father, although the guide had worked with Turghunbayeva as a dancer. In contrast with Avdeyeva's biographical account, the guide did say that Turghunbayeva started her dance career with her family's support. In any event, she became one of the most famous dancers of her generation and founded the nation's leading Uzbek dance company, the *Bahor* Ensemble.

In contemporary Uzbekistan, dancers and nondancers remember her most for the works she introduced to the Uzbek stage. The *Bahor* Ensemble has over 200 works in its active repertory, many attributed to Turghunbayeva or her contemporaries Tamara Khonim and the artist Usta Alim Kamilov. Her biography contains a chronological listing of many of the works she appeared in from 1929 until her death in 1978 (Avdeyeva 1989: 104–108).

Although dancers and nondancers recall Turghunbayeva primarily as a dancer, the museum tour guide and her biographer said that she also acted and sang. She appeared in *Örtoqlar* (*Comrades*), a musical comedy, as early as 1930. The titles of works she performed reflect Soviet themes and Central Asian life: *8 Marta* (March 8th) (1933), *Pakhta* (*Cotton*) (1933), *Ozodlik* (*Freedom*) (1949), and *Ghayratli Qiz* (*Energetic Girl*) (1955).

Others draw on Central Asian literature, such as *Farhod wa Shirin, Leila wa Majnun,* and *Munojot.* Still others express regional identities, such as *Bukharskii Raks.* It is fitting that she be represented here by one of the works she added to the repertoire of Uzbek classical dance.

The life of Mukarram Turghunbayeva is typical of the destiny of Uzbek women—it was progress to spiritual emancipation and it really did not matter what profession the women chose: weaver, biologist, teacher or actress. Turghunbayeva's artistic career was indeed unique. It had tremendous bearing on the destinies of Uzbek women, because it stimulated the development of an entirely new female personality. Every dance performed by Mukarram depicted life as it was. At the same time the plasticity of the dance expressed the new spiritual features of the women of her time. (Avdeyeva 1989: 198)

Although Turghunbayeva died in 1978, I was able to interview a woman, Shirin, who had been a close friend of Turghunbaycva's for decades. Shirin was the wife a member of the intelligentsia. I attended her son's wedding. The day after the festivities were over, we sat at her kitchen table while soup for lunch simmered on the stove. As we talked, her daughter joined us, adding her own impressions and childhood memories of Turghunbayeva. She and Turghunbayeva met during an extended stay in the hospital. I asked what Turghunbayeva was like. Shirin said:

Mukarram *opa*[4] and I were together in the hospital in the year 1968 in Tashkent. Twenty-four days. She was a very very good woman. That woman was never tired. In order for a [festival?] ensemble to flourish, even when she was in bed in the hospital she always participated in rehearsals. Later on when we lived in *** province, *opa* came to *** province. Forty days they gave concerts at our place every day. We met together every day. That woman was never tired. With her own company she was an affectionate friend [*ulfat*] to the girls.

Shirin learned much from watching and performed her own version of *"Tanovar"* at a social event she hosted. As discussed in greater detail below, *"Tanovar"* is perhaps the greatest of Turghunbayeva's works and has become a quintessential example of Uzbek national dance. I saw a fragment of Shirin's dance. Compared to the cheerful lightness of the other women who danced that day, Shirin moved with focussed intention, pressing through movements as though she were moving through "thick space."[5]

MD: You dance *"Tanovar"* yourself.

Shirin: I dance [my own version]. I dance mine . . . I heard Muhammadjon Mirzaev during our time in the hospital. He even had *Munojot, "Tanovar"* played. During the playing, *opa* danced. Whatever she was doing, every day in the morning for forty-five minutes she would occupy herself so that weight gain would not come, or whatever would not come. While she was occupied this way during [her] time of staying [in the hospital] if there was some music she would occupy herself with dancing. Afterwards I would dance too. When I danced "so you will dance Andijon style and I will dance Parghana style," she said. At home we Andijonese a little mmmmm. Ssssst! there is speed. We dance faster. Very fast! [Jaaaah!]. . . . What did she say "in Parghana they dance slower." For this reason there were days she said, "You are making us all speed up." I learned a lot of things from *opa*.

MD: You do a terrific *"Tanovar."*

Shirin (chuckling): We learned a little *tanovar* from that Mukarram *opa*!

MD: I would like to learn it.

Shirin: So that was how it was.

I asked Shirin to tell me some stories about Turghunbayeva. "What kind of stories?" she responded. So I asked her to tell me what they did during the forty days Turghunbayeva visited Shirin's province.

Together, those forty days in the time when the ensemble came. We would be together from morning until dinner. Respect for *opa* was so great that in Z*** province . . . in Z*** province there were only one or two Andijonese, Tashkentese people. All of the rest were Z*** province people. So greatly had *opa* found a way to the hearts of people that every day for forty days she was made a guest. One after the other one day at our place, one day at yet another place she was made a guest. . . . She was a very fabulous teacher.

I told Shirin that books in America mention Tamara Khonim rather than Turghunbayeva. I asked why Turghunbayeva is more well-known in Uzbekistan than Tamara Khonim. Shirin thought a moment and replied:

Mukarram *opa's* dances are closer to the Uzbek people than Tamara Khonim's. Tamara Khonim is more known for her foreign dances. Mukarram *opa* took Uzbek folk dances as the basis for her dances.

"TANOVAR"[6]

Of all the works Turghunbayeva performed, perhaps the most enduring is *"Tanovar."* Viewing the dance *"Tanovar"* as a kind of ethnography, it is a work that weaves together themes of national identity, complicity and resistance to Soviet reforms, and changing norms about gender. The significance of *"Tanovar"* in Uzbek culture cannot be overstated. Avdeyeva considered it

one of the masterpieces of Soviet choreography. This single-act national ballet is so inspired and poetical in nature that prominent artistes, art directors and ballet masters compare Mukarram Turghunbayeva's *"Tanovar"* with the gem of world choreography "The Dying Swan" by M. Fokine. (1989: 199)

In 1994, professional dancers spoke of it reverently. Echoing the comments of Turghunbayeva's friend Shirin, the introduction to a book about

"Tanovar," published in 1994, described the dance as expressing emotional themes important in a woman's life:

The dance of *"Tanovar"* which has long blossomed on the Uzbek stage is closely entwined with the name of Mukarram Turghunbayeva. It is as if *"Tanovar"* is a large part of the life of Mukarram *opa:* love, longing, hope, parting. Everything wept over, felt, experienced will become *tanovar.* (Karimova 1993: 3)

Dancers consider *"Tanovar"* an ultimate test of a dancer's dramatic ability and artistry. One teacher identified the dances she would include in a program to teach me Uzbek dance. After learning a dance in the Farghana, Bukhara, and Khorezm styles, she would include a dance from another region, perhaps Uyghur and *doira dars* (a dance teaching a basic lexicon of movements and rhythms). "Then" she said, pausing dramatically, *"Tanovar."*

The dance also seemed to have a powerful effect on popular imaginations. Three women I met, two from a region near the Farghana Valley and one from the capital city of Tashkent, had created their own dance versions of *"Tanovar."* This well loved Uzbek classic might thus be considered one of the most "Uzbek" of the national dances.

"Tanovar" was created in 1943 and was first performed at the Alisher Navoi State Academic Theater of Opera and Ballet in the capital city of Tashkent. Turghunbayeva had heard that a dancer named Bidonkhon had presented a successful dance set to *"Tanovar."* Working with Evgenii Nikolaevich Baranovskii, the ballet master of the Alisher Navoi Theater, Turghunbayeva decided to stage her own version (Karimova 1993: 7). The music used in *"Tanovar"* is from the Farghana Valley region. When I asked a musician to play *"Tanovar"* for me, she was puzzled. "Which one?" she asked. I learned that for musicians *"Tanovar"* is a genre of folk music from the Farghana Valley region. There are many songs known as *"Tanovar"* and many variations on these melodies. Musicians have told me that it is ancient.

I attended a concert in Tashkent in honor of Mukarram Turghunbayeva's birthday (May 31). The concert was held at a music conservatory. The performers were teenaged dancers and musicians from an institute in the Farghana Valley who were studying to become teachers. The ensemble consisted of fifteen musicians and twelve female dancers. The instruments and gender of the musicians were as follows:

2 *doira* (tambourine) players	male
10 chordophone (stringed instrument) players	9 male
	1 female
2 *nay* (flute) players	male
2 *dutar* (long-necked, stringed instrument) players	female

The program notes handed out to the audience listed eight kinds of *"Tanovar."* A musician seated next to me explained that there were a total of fifteen kinds of *"Tanovar."* Each kind of *"Tanovar"* was a different variation of a single musical motif. The names of the eight *"Tanovars"* performed for the concert were:

1. *"Gulbahor Tanovar"* (Spring Flower *Tanovar*)
2. *"Adolat Tanovari"* (The *Tanovar* of Adolat)[7]
3. *"Farghana Tanovari"* (The *Tanovar* of Farghana)
4. *"Mukimii Gazali"* (Verse of [the poet] Mukimii)
5. *"Tanovar Janga His Eksam"* (*Tanovar* [of Emotion?])
6. *"Sunbulla Tanovari"* (*Tanovar* of Sunbula [8th month of the Arab calendar, August 22–September 21])
7. *"Tanovar II"*
8. *"Tanovar"*

Each *"Tanovar"* sounded quite different to me. In my fragmentary simultaneous notes, I heard at least four different rhythms, some using patterns of three beats, others of four beats. Tempi varied from slow and stately to rapid. Some were instrumental pieces, others featured a female vocalist or monophonic chorus of female voices. Dancers performed to each musical variation. The final *"Tanovar"* was the dance masterpiece Turghunbayeva made famous.

The movement motifs come from a regional style, which is known as the "Farghana style." Dancers say that it uses folk dance motifs from the Farghana Valley region. There are three major professional dance styles, one for each of the three major oases of Farghana, Bukhara, and Khorezm. It is significant that the music and movements are supposed to originate from the Farghana Valley. Farghana is the birthplace of many of the nation's best musicians, and considered a place where people are highly civilized and love the arts. The musical and movement motifs represent a major political region and evoke memories of great cultural achievements.

A retired dancer gave me a tape of a television program about *"Tanovar."* The tape includes a black and white movie of Turghunbayeva. A scrolled arch hangs over the stage suggesting an arch of flowers or perhaps the overhanging branches of trees. One male singer in the traditional Uzbek dress of a *chöpon* (a striped silk long-sleeved robe) and a *döppi* (a square embroidered cap) accompanies himself on a long-necked, fretted chordophone, probably a *dutar*. His voice is clear and resonant but the words are unintelligible to me because the syllables are distorted by melisma and a throbbing vibrato.

Some fifteen women are seated on the floor around the sides and back of the stage in companionable tableaus. The women wear the regional dress of the Farghana region—open collared, long smocks made of an ikat-patterned silk called *atlas*. Many people told me that *atlas* is the "national" fabric of Uzbekistan, or that clothing made of *atlas* is "national" dress.[8] Scarves or *döppilar* covered the women's heads, in keeping with Muslim norms requiring women to dress modestly. The women's voices alternated with the male soloist's in a call and response pattern. The women echoed motifs in the man's solo by a high, nasal monophonic chorus. One woman stands playing a *doira*. A *nay* repeated motifs from the man's solo, although the camera never clearly showed the *nay* player. The tempo was brisk and asymmetric, led by the *doira* in the following pattern:

Turghunbayeva enters from stage right and moves upstage with tiny skimming steps. She turns to the camera and bows with her right hand over her heart. The pause gives me a moment to see that she too wears the traditional dress of the Farghana Valley region: a scarf tied into a cap, knee-length braids, a shimmering ankle-length robe open over a white caftan and pants gathered at the ankle. A glittering metallic necklace, earrings, and bracelets complete the ensemble. She looks directly into the camera with a confident smile. Her gestures are bold, direct, and strong.

She sights into the distance, one hand held horizontally across her chin, palm facing the floor. Her head turns to the right and down, looking at the floor. (I wonder if she is being coy, or if she is unhappy.) She glides sideways, slowly drawing clenched fists up the sides of her body as though containing an explosion. With a cocky tilt of her head and a sparkle in her eyes, she shoves up the sleeves of her gown, exposing her wrists. Shaking her head, she claps her hands as though brushing dust away. As the *doira* accelerates, she raises both arms overhead and slowly pivots, snapping her fingers in rapid counterpoint. The music slows as she completes the turn and Turghunbayeva swirls into a gracious bow accompanied by a final trill of the *nay*.

Turning to narrative content, *"Tanovar"* tells the story of a young girl who is waiting for her sweetheart in a garden. The lyrics express the bittersweet joy of love and the pain of longing and separation. The dancer's gestures illustrate the words. For example, the dancer slowly raises her clenched fists up the sides of her body and over her head to express discouragement when her lover does not appear, then reaches forward, palms up, when she thinks that she sees him in the distance.

According to Karimova (1987), women perform *"Tanovar"* using folk texts. One version (in Karimova 1987) by a female singer is as follows:

> Your gaze is the axis of my world
> Your Adolat [Justice], I shall be,
> When my black hair grew, upon my brow it curled,
> Your living sacrifice, I shall be,
> What woes bow my head,
> Your willing sacrifice, I shall be
> Before your love, my freedom fled
> Your devoted slave, I shall be
> While flames blaze from my body, my heart smolders,
> Your fervent pilgrim [dervish], I shall be
> I from you, and you from me, may we never part,
> Your Adolat, I shall be . . .

Men, however, also performed their own renditions of *"Tanovar."* Karimova (1987) said:

Male singers [reciters], however, perform the following musical ghazal of the Uzbek democratic poet Mukimii in the style of *"Tanovar"*:

> To find a beautiful, beautiful woman like you, any journey I will brave
> When a rose sees your face it becomes your slave,
> As long as my soul is in my body, may it be love's enclave
> Everywhere I am, with you my heart stays
> In our souls the flame of your love burst into light
> For khans and for kings I care not a mite
> As a tulip blooms, my heart brims with delight
> Everywhere I am, with you my heart stays.

Comparing these examples of female and male versions of *"Tanovar"* suggests sharp differences in gender norms. The woman's verses depict a woman as martyred by love, and love as the end of freedom. By contrast, a male version shows love as the end of a heroic journey. The male version celebrates the man's agency and autonomy, and his enjoyment of a woman's beauty. The few words I can understand on the videotape ("my great love") do not correspond to any of the verses Karimova quotes in her article, so I do not know whether the singer is performing a male or female variant of the song.

The dance and music touch on many themes that resonate deeply in Uzbek culture: the reputation of the Farghana Valley as the birthplace of the nation's finest musicians, and the loveliness and soulful depth of Uzbek women. The dance also delivers messages pertinent to Soviet policy of the period. The Farghana Valley was, and remains, the region of Uzbekistan where Islamic devotion is the strongest. *"Tanovar"* thus uses the beloved music of the Valley to accompany a public performance by a female dancer, a use directly opposed to the Muslim values held by the Valley residents.

Karimova observed that the theme of romantic love was important in many pieces during the 1930s. She also said that the dancers performed in order to show people "how they should act." I suspect that dramatizing the theme of romantic love challenged the Central Asian Muslim practice of arranging marriages. *"Tanovar"* thus links indigenous pride in culture and beauty with modern Soviet notions of nationhood, choice, and independence.

LIVING FOR ART

Looking at the early dancers' life histories together with *"Tanovar"* shows the ambiguous place of Uzbek dance and dancers in Uzbek society. Tamara Khonim, Roziya Karimova, and Mukarram Turghunbayeva each established a vital dimension of national dances as an institution. Tamara Khonim took the first bold step of dancing in public without a veil. With her husband Kari Yakubov, she helped to launch Uzbekistan's first professional performing ensemble. Through her international touring, she helped to bring recognition to Uzbek dance and music as an art form.

Moreover, she trained the first group of young dancers, including Roziya Karimova. Karimova considers Tamara Khonim her teacher (*usta*). In teaching young girls at the choreographic school today, she continues to transmit the training exercises and combinations of steps and rhythm she learned from Tamara Khonim. Mukarram Turghunbayeva founded the nation's leading dance company. As a director and a dancer, she added many new works to the repertoire of Uzbek professional dance. In 1994 the *Bahor* Ensemble had over 200 works in its active repertory, many created or popularized by Turghunbayeva.

The personal lives of these women also showed the ambiguous impact of Soviet reforms on the lives of individual women. On the one hand, the establishment of dance as a career increased the life choices available to women. Tamara Khonim, according to the museum tour guide, chose dance over her parents' objections. All three women, with the position and financial resources afforded by their own careers, divorced and remarried. Tamara Khonim also resourcefully combined the traditional path of marriage and the new Soviet option of a career through marrying Kari Yakubov, her director and one of the country's leading musicians. Turghunbayeva married the famous musician Kamilov.

Marriage to a musician and fellow performing ensemble member alleviated problems of propriety. In Uzbekistan, as in many Muslim societies, the honor of the men in a family depends upon the virtue of their women (see, e.g., Abu-Lughod 1993). The daughter of a woman who began dancing in the 1930s told me that her father recruited her mother as a professional performer by marrying her. In 1994 several dancers told me that marrying a musician is still the ideal option for a female dancer. "If your husband is a musician, then he is always with you when you are working or traveling. No one can criticize you then." No one could gainsay the husband's authority to allow his wife to perform, nor could anyone accuse her of immoral conduct while working or traveling because she would always be under his watchful eye.

On the other hand, appearing on stage, even with spousal approval and supervision, drastically lowered a woman's social standing. I met a venerable and devout elderly gentleman in a rural village. He cheerfully told me about famous dancers like Tamara Khonim. They had come to the Farghana Valley and he had seen them dance. I asked him what people had thought about the dancers in the 1930s. With some reluctance, he finally admitted, "We didn't like them much then."

One night on television I saw an old black and white tape of Tamara Khonim dancing. Smiling widely, eyes flashing, she moved on a little patch of dusty earth, ringed on three sides by men with leathery, seamed faces shining with oil and perspiration. *Döppilar* clung to their heads, and *chöpons* hugged their bodies. Tamara Khonim skimmed the ground in little steps, snapped her fingers, spun, and finally dropped to her knees. She arched her back until her head nearly touched the ground.

As I watched, I grew increasingly uncomfortable. After months in the field, I had learned to drop my eyes when passing men on the street and to avoid eye contact when introduced. The men's eyes on Tamara Khonim were too direct. The smiles on their faces stretched into toothy grimaces. I suddenly realized how very shocking the early dancers must have seemed. I wondered how the dancers felt appearing on the stage day after day. Perhaps this was why every dancer I had met discreetly wore a black and white bead tucked in her clothing to ward off the evil eye.

In the 1930s, how did dancers view their work? Karimova told me:

At that time I was young. I did not think about freedom or whatever it was called . . . I lived for art. I lived for the dance. I danced for the sake of art and for the dance. So I did not think about the emergence of freedom or those things. It was my youth. I did not think about it. Who would think about politics? Only later on there were dances made which related to freedom. Dances began to appear which were connected to freedom for women. In 1935 when they threw off the *paranji* [veils] our problems were depicted in dances which came out.

Concerts [*spektaklar*] came out, came out. Full-length spectacles. From the problems of the emerging of this freedom for women and girls . . . there is the spectacle of Noor Khon. Noor Khon was murdered because she was a performer. Noor Khon is a story of Farghana. There the sister of Noor Khon is alive. She lives in Tashkent. She is very ill. . . . She is close to ninety. She was from Farghana. She was the wife of Usta Alim. They were artists. She was called Begimkhon. . . . That Begimkhon was the younger sister of Noor Khon. Noor Khon was murdered for becoming an artist. Her father's son by another wife stabbed her with a knife in eighteen places. They wanted to kill Begimkhon too. They invited her as a guest. But when her

older sister unexpectedly fell ill, she could not go as a guest. For this reason they
did not kill her. After the father gave her elder brother vodka, and gave him a
Quran, and made him swear, this little sister has taken a bad road. She has become
a nonbeliever [*kaffir*], that is to say, bad. "If you don't kill her it will be a sin," said
her father. [Her father] having forced him, this [brother] killed Noor Khon.

Noor Khon was earlier than me. Begimkhon's younger sister came to Tashkent
[correcting herself] Samarkhand at the theater where everyone came together.
Usta Alim took Beghimkhon in marriage. And so some time later they were going
to go to Farghana. They themselves were from Farghana. That older brother there
caused her death. When they went on tour in Farghana, her older sister and
mother invited her as a guest. That's when he killed her. There [was a big party?
and] some other girls there. When they were dancing Noor Khon's older brother
invited her into the garden. "You are staying. You will wear a *paranji*," he said.
"You will not be an artist." "No, I will be an artist," she said. He killed her. "Ah,
you will become an artist?" he said. She was killed. This is how it was.

This became a spectacle. . . . They killed her father. . . . They imprisoned her
older brother. He was young and he didn't know. He said her father compelled
me. He went to war. In 1941. He came back from the war. After he returned he
himself got married. Even though he was a little ill. He got married, her older
brother.

Veiling in Muslim societies is a topic that has been addressed by anthropologists as well as scholars in other disciplines (see, e.g., Fernea
[1965] 1989; Beck and Keddie 1978; Abu-Lughod 1986; Tohidi 1991; Badran, 1995). A practice associated with women of upper classes during Muhammad's lifetime, veiling is not required under Islam. The Quran
enjoins men and women to dress "modestly."

Karimova's account of Noor Khon's death associates veiling with con-
troversies over Muslim and Soviet norms for women, and new freedoms
offered under the Soviet system. The associations of veiling and "backward" ways, and unveiling and progress were strongly marked in a museum I visited. The museum displayed a *paranji* as part of an exhibit about
modernization and improvements introduced during the Soviet period.
The long, black, coarse robe covered the mannequin's form from head
to toe, with a grid of strips of fabric over the eyes. It looked harsh, hot,
and confining, like a portable jail with bars. Another part of the exhibit
showed photographs of a long river worm that could enter bare feet, an
affliction eliminated by Soviet intervention. Urban women grimaced at
rumors circulating in 1994 that veiling might return, and looked at the
practice as backward and a threat to their freedom.

As the first woman to dance unveiled in public, Tamara Khonim was
part of a larger Soviet program to bring women into the workplace and
to give them greater authority in the home through measures such as
greater access to divorce. Her unveiling violated Central Asian norms of

respectability. The tragedy of Noor Khon's death shows that performing on the stage challenged men related to a dancer, whose honor depended upon her respectability. Controversial in terms of Muslim Central Asian values, dancing was part of a larger program of "modernization" aimed at creating a public sphere for women.

By the end of the Soviet period, Mukarram Turghunbayeva had become a heroic pioneer. Her biographer praised her for founding Uzbek dance:

> It may be stated as a fact that Mukarram Turghunbayeva had created the Uzbek stage dance—an entirely new type of art in Uzbek musical culture. It was as new as the symphony, opera and classical ballet were to Uzbekistan. Mukarram Turghunbayeva adopted the innovatory methods of the first Uzbek Soviet choreographers. . . . Usta Alim Kamilov, who knew all the fine points of Uzbek folk and professional dance, remained her friend and co-author to the last days of his life. This helped Mukarram Turghunbaeva [sic] to make all her scenic productions freshly new and yet typically Uzbek. (Avdeyeva 1989: 198–199)

CONCLUSION

Anthony Giddens (1984) offers the attractive model of dialectics between structure and agency. He analyzes some of the ways in which structures constrain and enable actors, and how individual choices, in turn, create structure. The contributions and lives of the early Uzbek dancers can, in part, be explained in terms of complex dialectics between structure and agency. Although Giddens' model partially helps to explain the impact of the first national dancers on the establishment of Uzbek national dances, and of the Soviet reforms on the dancers themselves, it leaves out the crucial dimensions of cooperation and resistance.

National dances were constructions of the new Soviet consciousness, combining the separate power bases of Bukhara, Khorezm, and Farghana. Moreover, they brought women out of the private domestic sphere into the public one. Through performing works such as "Tanovar" and in their personal lives, the dancers exemplified the privileges and perils of becoming "modern" Soviet women. Tamara Khonim and Roziya Karimova's life histories and the dance "Tanovar" illustrate the ambiguity and paradoxes of Uzbek dance. Women were at once oppressed, implicated, and freed by the Soviet colonial program. On the stage, the dancers became living emblems of the new SSR of Uzbekistan. The dances and dancers thus became emblems of the new political regime and social order. Their pioneering work established an enduring centralized institutional framework for national dances.

James Scott (1990) identifies overt and covert forms of resistance. Incorporating questions about power into an analysis of Uzbek dance shows that although Tamara Khonim, Roziya Karimova, and Mukarram Turghunbayeva participated in Soviet programs to make Central Asia conform to a Soviet mold, they also helped to develop an institution that celebrated and preserved the legacies of the sophisticated cultures of Bukhara, Farghana, and Khorezm. Did Uzbek national dancers and musicians allow treasured art forms to become vehicles of Soviet propaganda, or did they use Soviet resources to help vital portions of Central Asia's artistic heritage?

NOTES

1. Making the pilgrimage to Mecca (*hajj*) at least once during one's lifetime is one of the five obligations of an observant Muslim. A *hajji* is a person who has made the pilgrimage.

2. Teachers used the term "waltz" (*vals*) to request music for Farghana dances from the musicians accompanying class, or to tell students to demonstrate the Farghana dance they had learned for class. The term is the one used by Uzbek dance teachers and not one I have imposed upon the music or dance form.

3. A *dutar* is a long-necked, stringed instrument. I met women who played the *dutar* as a hobby. Women musicians who played for weddings or onstage for concerts were more rare, although I did meet a few. I do not know whether Turghunbayeva's mother was an amateur or professional musician.

4. *Opa* literally means "elder sister," but is used as a term of respect for women older than the speaker.

5. Anya Peterson Royce (1984: 70–71, 77) describes moving through "thick space" as one of the characteristics of mime. The "weightedness" of the mime's movements are a distinctive characteristic of mime technique, in contrast to ballet where dancers strive to achieve the illusion of weightlessness.

6. I asked one Uzbek arts scholar what the word *tanovar* meant. She speculated that it could have two meanings: first, that one should accept God's will, or second, that it referred to the words for "body" (*tan*) and "to bring something" (*ob kelmok*).

7. *Adolat* literally means "justice." In this context it is probably the name of a female singer named Adolat famous for singing a *"Tanovar"* as discussed below.

8. See Chapter 4 for a discussion of a new bride's dowry, which consists of both modern (*sovremnii*) and national (*millii*) clothing. Women in the Farghana Valley used to weave their own *atlas* fabric at home for their families or for sale in the bazaar. One family I met in the Farghana Valley said they would help me to find some homemade *atlas*, but our plans never materialized. Women in Tashkent said that Marghilon, a region in the Farghana Valley, was famous for its *atlas*. Although some women still make *atlas* themselves, I visited a women's cooperative factory where workers made *atlas* on machines.

Many fabric patterns exist and have colorful names such as peacock, comb, and chess. The peacock pattern is primarily blue, black, white, and green shot with gold threads. It is considered a *qora* (black) *atlas* whose darker colors make it suitable for mature women. One wife of a professor in Tashkent who knew I was in my late thirties told me that I was old enough to wear *qora atlas*. Yellow (*saruk*) *atlas* was for women in their twenties and early thirties. Women told me fabric dominated by red was for younger women. I noticed women actually wore yellow and red *atlas* well into middle and even old age. *Atlas* was a correct and substantial gift to any girl or woman. Brides and young women received three meters—enough for a short-sleeved, calf-length dress. Five meters was appropriate for mature women so they could make a long-sleeved dress. When I left Uzbekistan in December of 1994, *atlas* cost about 100 to 150 som per meter, about two week's salary.

3

The War Years: "We Made Dance a Beautiful Diamond" (circa 1943–1953)

With the onset of World War II, Uzbeks participated in the effort to unite all of the peoples of the Soviet Union. If the task of the 1930s was building a national consciousness from the disparate tribal and ethnic groups located within the borders of the new SSR of Uzbekistan, the task of the 1940s and 1950s was building a pan-Soviet consciousness. When Russia entered World War II, Uzbeks were called into service. Men went into the military, while dancers were recruited to entertain troops at the front. Russia's entry into World War II brought substantial changes to the organization and practice of national dances. All of the films and photographs I have seen of dances from the 1930s usually feature one or two dancers performing solos. The earliest ensemble work I saw dated from 1937. It resembled a military review with individuals formed into orderly, trained ranks.

It is likely that coordinated ensemble work in Uzbek dance developed during World War II.[1] Perhaps the early documentation of single performers I saw recorded only the most popular dances or performers such as Tamara Khonim or Mukarram Turghunbayeva. Alternatively, this change in emphasis may reflect key differences in context from the 1930s and the 1940s. In the 1930s, Soviet policy encouraged women to break away from their family obligations and Muslim values. Individual choice and independence were emphasized (Massell 1974: 133).

By contrast, in the 1940s, the Soviets needed to mobilize all the Soviet peoples first in support of Stalin's "Unholy Alliance" with Nazi Germany (1939–1941), and later to defend the USSR against German invasion (1941–1945). During the early years of the Soviet period and during World War II, dance was a channel of communication and a vivid emblem of the values the Soviets sought to instill in the Uzbek people.

In Uzbekistan programs for education (Allworth 1967), agricultural de-

velopment (Matley 1967a), and industrialization (Matley 1967b) were being established by the Soviet government. Examining the development of
schools and institutes of Uzbek dance affords insight into the methods
the Soviets used to permeate Uzbek society and the effect of these efforts
on at least a few specific individuals.

MILITARY SERVICE

Dancers who went to the front during World War II actually became
part of the military. One of Tamara Khonim's sisters led a dance company
that visited soldiers at the front during World War II. Roziya Karimova
(see Chapter 2) was one of the members of the troupe that toured the
front. I asked her where the dancers performed. She said little about this
period, merely replying with harsh pride, "We went to the front." She
proudly displayed her veteran's uniform that glittered with row after row
of medals. During my field research in 1994, she wore her uniform many
times both socially and for government-sponsored occasions. She said that
she was invited to many events because she was a veteran. During 1994
Karimova and a group of other veterans toured former Soviet Central Asia
and were honored for their service. The biography of Margarita Akilova,
a famous contemporary of Karimova's, described a tour to Iran in the
Spring of 1942 as follows:

In the months of April and May, under the leadership of Tokhtasin Jalilov, forty
Uzbek artists were in neighboring Iran. Renowned artists were in one row in the
famous brigade: the dramatic actors Sora Eshontoraeva and the late Olim Hojaeva,
side by side with the talented singers Ma'murjon Uzoqov, Zaynab Polvonova, and
skillful dancers such as Mukarram Turghunbayeva, Shahodat Rahimova, Roziya
Karimova, Fakhiya Jamilova, Tamara Nazarova, Jabijon Hasanov, and the late Jyr-
akhon Sultonov. For about a month and a half, this brigade performed razzmatazz
[rang-barang] programs for the workers of Iran and the Soviet soldiers and com-
manders stationed there.

From the ideological/creative perspective, the artists created works which would
answer the needs of the era, such as "Father of the Ages," "Sword of Uzbekistan,"
"Qochqor Turdiev" as musical works for stage, and the film "Gift for the Front."
Through building the Farhod GES, which was the monument recognizing the
heroism of the people during these kinds of tours, artists honored active service.
(Ahmedov 1985: 36)

One of the dances from the World War II period repertoire was revived
for the 1994 Independence Day Concert. It was choreographed in 1937
for Uzbek national dancers who went to the front in World War II to
perform for the soldiers. The woman in charge of restaging it for the
concert was Margarita Akilova's daughter. She learned the choreography
as a child when a dancer in her family went to the front. The movement

vocabulary was drawn from the Farghana Valley regional style, as were the costumes.

According to a music student who helped me as a research assistant, the music was a song called *"Yalla"* ("Let's Go"). The music was prerecorded so I could not identify the instruments or number of singers with precision. A large mixed chorus sang stanzas in a call and response pattern, alternating between male and female voices, then singing in unison. An orchestra dominated by flutes and drums echoed fragments of the melody. My assistant said the music was "an ancient folk song" from the Farghana Valley region. The lyrics were from a poem by the Central Asian poet Alisher Navoi (1441–1501).

The dance opened a portion of the concert that gave a capsule history of the late 1930s and World War II. Over thirty dancers entered in a square formation of rows and columns. The choreography had a martial theme, with the dancers marching in unison. The sharp rhythm marked by drums and flutes seemed like a call to action[2]:

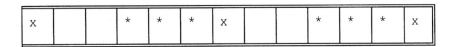

Their costumes were traditional dresses of the Farghana Valley—full-length, long-sleeved caftans, wine velvet boleros embroidered in gold thread, and white square caps with multicolored embroidery. The long dress with a bolero was a style of national dress associated with the 1920s and 1930s. More contemporary national dress for the region consisted of a dress ending a few inches below the knee, matching trousers gathered at the ankle (*lozim*), and no vest. The caftans were made of *atlas* (ikat-patterned fabric), in a black, yellow, green, white, and red pattern (see Chapter 2, note 8).

Row by row, the dancers split off into five groups forming tableaus in small circles. Each group melded back into a single line stretching across the stage, presenting the audience with the spectacle of a seemingly endless line of dancers stepping in perfect unison.

1994 was a time of tension among the ethnic groups living in Uzbekistan. With the fall of the Soviet Union, the meaning of "Uzbek" was heavily contested. Members of other ethnic groups, such as Russian and Korean, were citizens of Uzbekistan, but were they "Uzbek"? The dancers were from the five major professional dance companies in Tashkent. Two of the companies, *Shodlik* (Joy) and *Bahor* Ensembles, specialized in Uzbek dance. The other three companies had regional specialties, one in Bukharan (Tajik) dance, a second in Khorezmian dance, and the third in Uyghur dance. Khorezm is a province in Uzbekistan known for its dancers.

Uyghurs are an Uzbek-speaking group of Turkic descent who live in the Sinkiang region of the People's Republic of China. The line, therefore, provided an overarching idiom of unity, which subsumed the disparate regional identities of the dancers in 1994.

The dancers were followed by a skit reenacting the opening of a canal in the Farghana Valley, an event that occurred in 1939. An actor dressed as the first president of Uzbekistan stood side by side with a man in Russian military dress to cut a red ribbon inaugurating the canal. The building of the Great Farghana Canal was a point of pride for Uzbeks because it had been built in only forty-five days by about 180,000 Uzbek and Tajik laborers, with the assistance of engineers and technicians who were probably Russians (Allworth 1967: 294). The canal signified both the dedication and unity of the Uzbek people and a modernizing contribution to the nation's welfare by the Soviets. The celebrations for the canal opening were interrupted by the sound of bombs and strafing planes. Men set down their scythes and marched off to war.

I asked several performers in the concert what the dance was about. They answered with a shrug and told me that it had been included in the program just because it was from 1937. One artist explained that it was one of the last truly "Uzbek" dances.

Uzbekistan became a haven for refugees from Moscow displaced by the war and for artists exiled by Stalin. After World War II, these Russian-trained artists and critics influenced the arts in Uzbekistan, founding institutes for theatrical studies, choreographic schools, and taking leadership positions in the theater. Therefore, works created after World War II had a Russian influence. Although the dance had none of the dramatic appeal of "Tanovar" (see Chapter 2), it was chosen at least in part because of its non-Russian provenance. Ironically, the dance contains many motifs associated with Russian choreography of the period, such as tableaus of dancers kneeling around a central standing figure and a corps of dancers moving in single file through swirling formations. Despite the Russian influence visible in the piece, artists who discussed it with me in 1994 presented it as a "truly Uzbek" work.

In any event, the 1937 dance was a reminder of the heroism of Uzbek women dancers and male soldiers who had gone to the front in World War II. Since the audience of the Independence Day concert included many foreign dignitaries, the 1937 dance may also have affirmed Uzbekistan's right to take its place in the international community. An Uzbek friend who watched a tape of the concert with me was pleased with the section of the program about Uzbekistan's wartime service. With a satisfied nod, she said, "It's only right, we fought too."

The war front was not the only place dancers figured prominently in government-sponsored events. Newspapers from the late 1930s and early 1940s describe parades and massive celebrations held on Soviet holidays

such as International Worker's Solidarity Day (May 1) and the anniversary
of the October Revolution (November 7). For example, on May 1, 1941,
the year Germany invaded the Soviet Union, crowds filled the streets of
Samarkand.

A forest of banners, music and people filled the streets, the squares and the boul-
evards. Before the demonstration there was a parade. Leaders of the provincial
[*oblast*] party and Soviet organizations congratulated the workers. Over fifty thousand people participated in the demonstration. (Anonymous, *Qizil Özbekistan*,
1940)

I was told that the library archives in Tashkent contained no newspapers
for the years when the Soviet Union was actively engaged in World War
II, so I was not able to trace dancers' activities during the actual war years
through newspaper coverage. State-sponsored parades and other displays
were not unique to Uzbekistan but were held throughout the Soviet Union (Lane 1981). As Christel Lane (1981) extensively discusses, rituals
were an important element of Soviet political culture. Holidays such as
the anniversary of the October Revolution (November 7), Victory Day
(May 9), and International Women's Day (March 8) were marked by parades, household feasts, and concerts featuring performing artists and
sound and light shows. Cults of personality centered on leaders such as
Vladimir Lenin, Joseph Stalin, and Nikita Khrushchev were also distinctive
characteristics of Soviet politics.

INSTITUTIONALIZATION

The life histories of two women who began studying dance in the late
1930s are significant because they show the extent of institutionalization
of Uzbek dance that had occurred only a decade after Usta Alimov established Uzbekistan's first dance company. The first woman, whom I shall
call Dilorum, became a dancer. The second became a scholar interested
in culture. I will refer to her as Anna.

Turning first to recruitment, the women I interviewed studied dance
with their families' consent. Neither were orphans. Dilorum had dark hair
and eyes and appeared to be of Uzbek descent. Anna's origins were part
Turkic and part Russian. Her grandparents supported the Whites during
the Revolution and fled to Central Asia when the Whites were defeated.

Other well-known dancers from the period were the children of artists
and musicians. For example, in one family, both of the parents became
famous performers in the 1930s. Several of their children became equally
noted dancers.

Overall, the children who undertook dance training during the World
War II period were ethnically diverse, including Uzbeks, Bukharan Jews,

and Russians. Unlike Karimova's cohort, they were not recruited from orphanages; rather, they undertook dance studies voluntarily.

DILORUM

I met Dilorum at a children's *maktab* (school) where she teaches dance. We met in the teachers' lounge, a bustling room with sofas, armchairs, a desk, and a phone. Light flooded in through long windows. The high ceiling magnified sound: voices, the ringing telephone, and the busy clack of heels. I had come to observe whatever classes were meeting that day. Another teacher at the school introduced us explaining that Dilorum was a teacher and had been a *katta uyinchi* (great dancer) who performed both Russian ballet and Uzbek national dances. Dilorum smiled and turned her face modestly away, pleased with the extravagant praise. I do not know if the meeting had been arranged by our mutual friend, or occurred by chance. Our friend left to go teach a class, and Dilorum and I sat down on sofas, soon joined by another woman who spoke Russian.

I placed my tape recorder on the coffee table in front of us and began to tape our meeting. My tape recorder drew many interested glances. Other people seeing my tape recorder raised their voices even if they were speaking in groups across the room. People clustered in front of my lens whenever my camera was out. I found people crowding into the aural space of the tape as well, eager to register their presence.

The first part of the tape was a medley of voices, with frequent inter- jections by the Russian-speaking woman. Other voices at a distance wove in and out of the tape, often obscuring most of the conversation in our group on the sofas. People drifted away as classes began and I finally sat alone with Dilorum. I asked her if she was from Tashkent and she began to tell me her life story. Dilorum wore her black hair pulled back into a knob at the nape of her neck. Her plain black dress had a crisp lacy white collar. As we talked, her broad face lit up and her dark eyes sparkled. She was the daughter of politically influential members of the intelligentsia. Dilorum began studying dance at age seven when her mother took her to the ballet conservatory in Tashkent. She vividly remembered her very first class, taught by Usta Alimov. She energetically chanted the rhythm of the drum from the class while demonstrating the movements.

When World War II broke out, she was sent to Moscow along with other children who were considered particularly gifted. The children received dance training at the Bolshoi Ballet School. There she studied ballet (*klas- sikskii raks*). After winning prizes in an international youth competition in Moscow for both ballet and Uzbek dances, she joined a pan-Soviet com- pany. The company included singers from Kazakstan and "everywhere." Dancers included the great Russian ballerina Maya Plisetskaya. For the next twenty-five years[3] she toured with Soviet Union ensembles. She listed her extensive itinerary:

Dilorum: I was not in China. I was in Iran. I was in Afghanistan. I was in Burma. I was in Indonesia—Sukarno, invitation. . . . Then I was in Morocco, Tunis. When we continued traveling the continent—Tunis, Africa, Morocco, Sudan, Sudan. . . .

MD: Which roles did you play? Roles, dance . . .

Dilorum: Dance? Dance. *"Jonondon,"* Pamir dance, Khorezm dance and so on.

Russian-speaking teacher listening to conversation: Pamir dance [*Pamirskii*].

Dilorum: Pamir dance, Tajik dance.

Russian teacher: . . . *"Esmeralda."*

Dilorum: Let me think. . . .

Russian teacher: Pamir dance.

Dilorum: Yes.

Russian teacher: *"Tanovar."* . . .

After retiring with a pension, she taught outside of Uzbekistan, including Moscow. Soon, however, when her foot began to hurt she curtailed her travels.

So after coming to this place and giving lessons, then for two out of three years my foot ached. After coming to the People's Department and giving classes, I would leave. My foot hurt. Otherwise I wouldn't be in this place. I would have gone to America or someplace—a theater in Canada. There was work. There was a lot of work. I would have gone to Toronto. They invited me to Iran. After my foot became [chronically] unwell, I could not go anywhere.

Her speech was peppered with Russian words reflecting the many years she spent in Moscow. She married a scholar she met in Moscow through Mukarram Turghunbayeva's third husband. They had one child who works for the government. She had two grandchildren. I asked why so many women had to leave the stage when they married. She explained: "[They are] Uzbeks so they are Muslim."

ANNA

I interviewed Anna in the summer of 1992 in her office at the institute where she taught. We met through another professor at her institute who learned of my interest in dance. Anna understood some Uzbek but preferred to speak Russian. I spoke no Russian, so we spoke through translators, from Russian to Uzbek, and Uzbek to English.

Unfortunately, when I played back the tape of the interview, the Uzbek-speaking woman's soft voice was unintelligible. Yet another friend who spoke some English and fluent Russian gave me a rough oral translation of the interview while I took rapid notes of her broken English. For this reason, I have paraphrased Anna's remarks. Her experiences are significant to this discussion because they show how greatly dance recruitment changed by the 1940s. They also show the increased importance of formal training in the process of becoming a professional dancer. Anna studied dance as a child but did not become a dancer.

Anna started dancing as a young child in the Pioneer Palace in Tashkent. She fondly remembers Tamara Khonim as a very popular performer. Anna studied ballet, character, and Uzbek dance. She was among a group of students chosen for additional training because she had a special feeling for dance.

Anna's father was imprisoned shortly before World War II. She was not expelled from school because the administration of her school was also disrupted by political upheavals. When the war started, Anna was a teenager. She worked days in a factory. At night, she studied. When the war ended, she could not pursue a dance career because her training had been cut short by the war. She was told that she was too old to resume dance studies.

INSTITUTIONALIZATION OF DANCE

Comparing Dilorum and Anna's life histories shows how institutionalized dance recruitment and training had become. Dance training was available to children through the Pioneer Palace. Professional training with the most famous musicians and dancers of the time was also offered at the ballet conservatory in Tashkent. A newspaper article written by the renowned singer Halima Nasirova (1938) noted that in 1940 Uzbekistan had eighty-five theaters, a Philharmonia, a Conservatory, more than thirty music *maktab*, several *teknikums* (techincal schools), and a *klassikskii raks* (ballet) school. Direct ties with institutions in Moscow, such as the Bolshoi Ballet School, were also being established. Anna's frustrated dance career shows that dance had evolved into a profession requiring years of training.

When Dilorum retired from the stage, she taught dance in Uzbekistan and in other countries where the Soviets had political interests. Unable to pursue a career in dance, Anna chose academia. Stalin's oppressive policies and the war displaced many noted European and Russian scholars. These individuals helped to found institutes of higher education in Uzbekistan, one of which Anna attended. She studied with several leading professors from Moscow. After teaching at a *maktab* for several years, she began conducting independent research and became highly respected in her field. She was married and had one child who was also a scholar.

World War II was a pivotal period for the development of dance in Uzbekistan. Examining the kinds of changes that occurred suggests some of the channels through which Soviet power spread throughout Uzbek society, and the effect of these methods on at least two individual dancers. Anna's life history shows that by the end of World War II, dance training had become more extensive and that professional dancers had to meet fairly exacting standards by an early age. Training methods used in the 1940s and 1950s would be an area for further research. Listening to the dancers themselves, I conclude that dance training was a technique for embedding and forging a Soviet consciousness.

An important change in the discourse of the life histories occurs between the first Uzbek dancers and the dancers of the 1940s. When artists recalled the talents of the first Uzbek dancers, they used terms such as *tabii* (natural), *Hudo bergan* (God-given), or *yuragdan* (from the heart).

According to the biographies told in their museums, Tamara Khonim and Mukarram Turghunbayeva (see Chapter 2) were talented dancers as children. Each was recruited after a famous musician saw her dance. At least according to people I talked to in 1994, their abilities as dancers were considered more a result of innate talent rather than training. In contrast, by the 1940s talent was insufficient to become a dancer. Years of training were necessary as well.

Roziya Karimova (see Chapter 2), one of the early Uzbek dancers, spoke of Uzbek dance in terms of her very bones:

What shall I say. The richness of these Uzbek dances. Other nationalities also their own what do you call it [i.e., richness] of course. They have their own value. But during my childhood, my bones were formed and grew strong with those Uzbek national dances. I have danced Russian dances and Indian dances as well. I have danced many dances, but I love Uzbek dances more. Because [there is] poetry in it, how do I say it in Uzbek—innocent appeal [*muloyimlik*], dignity, beauty. Here, okay, it is just like a flower. It is just like a flower. If these people danced, the heart ached.

Dilorum was an early student of Turghunbayeva's. I asked her what Turghunbayeva used to tell dancers. According to Dilorum's recollections, a talent for Uzbek dance required being loved by "the people" (*khalq*) and physical coordination. The dancer had to be able to express "truth . . . from the heart" in every gesture.

MD: What advice did [Turghunbayeva] give to dancers?

Dilorum: To dancers? Beautiful dancing, doing each movement correctly. To be liked by the people. If she appeals to the people, it means she is a good dancer.

MD: [Laughing]

Dilorum: If she is happy when she sees the people, this girl will be a good dancer. Or, "if the people look at her like this and applaud weakly, this [girl] will not be a dancer" *opa* [elder "sister"] said. Heart is necessary. Heart. Heart—and coordi-

nation [*koordinatsiya*]. Coordination. Each movement must be correct [*toghri*]. . . .
Truth is from deep within the heart. . . . Every single gesture. Every single hand.
Every single nerve.

Dancing "from the heart" (*yuragdan*) was an expression conveying high
praise for a dancer's work. When I asked dancers for recollections of
Turghunbayeva, they rarely told personal anecdotes but said only that she
danced "from the heart." I heard both dancers and nondancers use the
expression when they admired a dancer.

The heart was also an important image in other contexts. A well-known
woman poet said that when she read her work on television, she spoke
"from her heart." The expression "having a good heart" (*yuragi yakhshi*)
also arose in conversation with a young single woman about the qualities
she hoped for in a husband. "From the heart" seemed to be a phrase
meaning sensitivity, integrity, honesty, and eloquence. Perhaps this char-
acterization of the early dancers legitimized Uzbek dance as a spontaneous
and authentic expression of Uzbek spirit.

The young women who became dancers in the 1940s, however, had to
complete years of formal training. As Anna's life history shows, talent and
a feeling for dance were no longer sufficient to launch a professional
career. A professional dancer was an individual who had developed a repertoire of skills through completing a prescribed program of training.

Dilorum assessed the differences between the early dancers in the 1930s
and her cohort in the 1940s as follows:

MD: One of our scholars says that women's lives changed during the Soviet period.
Is his talk accurate?

Dilorum: It's true. It's true. The scholar's talk is true. Why is it true? Because when
there was no Soviet state [*hukumat*], women and girls, you, me, and others, [stayed
in] the women's quarters in the home [*ichgari*] and wore the veil [*paranji*]. You
could only see the pupils of our eyes, and nothing else. All of us. Later there was
dance in the what do you call it. It was in the women's quarters. *"Tanovar"* was
[danced] in the [unmarried] girls' quarters. The *doira*—ra ta tum ta tum ta tum.
[*"Tanovar"*] originated in the women's quarters. Later when there was a Soviet
state, after everyone tore their *paranjis*, they became equal, equal, equal. And so
women, Muslims, and for example me, were very covered up, their hands were
like so . . . uuuh free. . . .

Then their dances too became free. Having come out from the women's quarters and become happy, they became free. Then pretty young girls who came out
of the women's quarters were free so they danced. For that reason it is true that
for example during the thirties Roziya *opa*, Mukarram *opa*, and Tamara *opa* became
free with their coming outside. Or as for *us*—[she names herself and three other
dancers]—*we* were already trained. We became professional. We were able to study
everything. From that we made dance a beautiful diamond. We learned to make
it a diamond. In the nineteen forties.

I asked Dilorum whether she was aware, in the 1940s, of the political implications of dance for women. She responded by discussing the examples set by her teachers, the importance of training, and the professional status of dancers. Reviewing the transcript below, I wonder now whether we slightly miscommunicated. Nevertheless, my strong impression during the interview was that she understood my question very well and was, in essence, saying that in the 1940s the dancers understood that they were examples for other women. For that reason they could not use the small and timid gestures untrained women used in indigenous dances. Instead, the dancers had to become larger than life by transforming the small gestures of indigenous folk dance into the broad, bold gestures of professionally trained artists.

MD: In the nineteen forties, did you know that you were a second cohort and that you worked for the freedom of women? At that time did you know? In the nineteen forties. Did you know that this example [*misol*]. . . ?

Dilorum: Ah, Ah. The example taught in school in the nineteen forties. I know that I will graduate a good dancer. Mukarram *opa* is teaching me. Usta Alim is teaching me. Roziya *opa* is teaching me. I know that mu . . . muslim this [unintelligible] will not work. For example ra ta ra ta [beginning to dance, seated in her chair] when I have become a professional, ra da in what way . . . how is it in English—[switches to Uzbek] broad, broad. Dance must be broad like this. Those years of the nineteen thirties—the stages, the stages [*tstele*] were tiny. Tiny. The clubs[4] were tiny. The theater Navoi[5] was large. So in those places on the stage long [movements—she gestures with her arms, reaching and looking out in the distance], presence, presence—the movement did not have to be affected [*manmanlik*]. The movement had to be (*ja!*) very much like this. [She extends her left arm as though saluting an audience in the highest balcony.] So people would be seen. Professionally [*profetsionalnii*]. School [*shkola*]. School [*maktab*]. The fundamentals must be [learned in] school.

DANCE TRAINING

By the 1940s, then, training was essential to becoming a professional national dancer. Most of the dancers in the major companies in Tashkent were graduates of a children's choreographic *maktab*. The school where I observed classes offered a five-year program in Uzbek national dance and an eight-year program in ballet, along with academic classes. The school had a dormitory (*internat*) for children from regions outside of Tashkent. Some of the dancers I interviewed left their families and came to the school as early as age ten, others did not begin until their early teens.

A brief digression on the educational system in Uzbekistan will provide a context for the discussion of dance training and clarify terms used throughout the life histories. From the ages of one to six, children may attend a *boghcha* (day-care center). A *maktab* educates children from ages seven to seventeen. Within the *maktab*, distinctions may exist between the *boshlanghich* (beginning classes) for ages seven to ten, and the *örta maktab* (middle school) for ages ten to seventeen. An *olii maktab* (high school) refers either to a college or to fifteen to seventeen year olds in a *maktab*.

After attending a *maktab*, students may continue their studies at a *teknikum* or an *institut* (technical institute). At a *teknikum*, from age fifteen, students may receive four to five years of training in music or in service fields such as nursing or special education. An *institut* offers five years of higher education for students beginning at age seventeen. Tashkent boasts many institutes in fields such as history (*tarukh*), Eastern languages (*shark shunoslik*), world languages (*jahon tili*), and the arts (*san'at*).

Returning to the choreographic *maktab*, what did dancers learn in dance classes? Although I did not elicit detailed accounts of training methods used in the 1940s, I did observe classes and examinations at a choreographic school in Tashkent during the spring of 1994. The school trained and evaluated the students according to many standards, including knowledge of the prescribed syllabus, talent, and ethnic appearance.

The first book codifying Uzbek dance technique was written in 1965 and published eight years later (Karimova 1973). Since then Roziya Karimova, a noted dancer, teacher, and scholar, has published a series of books carefully documenting and codifying the distinctive movement motifs of the Farghana (1973), Bukhara (1977), and Khorezm (1975) dance styles.

The curriculum for the school was set by Moscow, even in 1994 after Uzbekistan declared independence from the Soviet Union. The children learned a five-year curriculum. They studied during the year with other children in the same level of the curriculum. Within each class, they were further divided by gender and by their concentration in ballet or Uzbek dance. Ethnic origin appeared to have at least some correlation with the kind of dance a student studied. Most of the students studying ballet had fair hair and complexions associated with Russian descent. By contrast, only one student concentrating in Uzbek dance was blond with fair skin. The other Uzbek dance students usually had dark hair, brown eyes, and more olive-toned complexions indicating that they were probably at least part Uzbek. In 1994 students specializing in Uzbek dance nevertheless studied ballet every day and Uzbek dance two days per week.

Within the Uzbek dance classes, students were grouped by age and ability. Although the content of their course work was similar, the children in one group had been described to me as a "good" group, and the other as a "bad" group. In observing classes during examinations and the semester, I noticed that the "good" group generally learned quickly, paid attention in class, and had long arms and straight limbs and backs and strikingly pretty faces. Their physical coordination was smooth and graceful, and their understanding of the complex and subtle rhythms of Uzbek music was generally acutely accurate.

By contrast, the "bad" students, appeared less alert, forgot movement sequences, moved more awkwardly, and some appeared sallow or even sickly. The two classes also elicited different responses from the same instructor. The "good" group received smiles, praise, and technical corrections such as demonstrations of proper timing of the footwork on turns. The "bad" group received criticism, scoldings, and sour looks. I was told these students would return to the provinces to teach after graduation instead of performing with companies in Tashkent.

I will describe one class I videotaped, then compare it with several others I observed. The girls were about ten years old and at the second-year level. The class was held in a large room with mirrors lining one wall and a wooden floor with splintering, uneven boards. Ballet barres ran the length of the room underneath grimy windows with cracked panes. Even wearing a heavy cardigan sweater I was cold. The students wore black leotards, knee-length black or white skirts and ballet slippers. Their hair was pulled into tidy round buns at the crown of their heads. When they spun, their skirts swirled out like skating skirts. Most wore white socks rather than tights. When I entered with the teacher, a former national dancer, the class lined up in three lines facing the mirrors. They began with three bows, one toward the teacher standing at the front of the room, one to the musicians at the side, and, prompted by their teacher, to me as a guest. Two male musicians—a gray-haired *dutar* player and a middle-aged *doira* player accompanied the class.

The students had memorized all of the sequences they performed in class, so the lesson consisted of performing set exercises. The teacher would offer some corrections or advice, then the dancers would perform the dance again or review a particularly difficult portion several times. The dancers started slowly, reviewing *holat* (the seven positions of the arms and feet), moving into a series of exercises to develop suppleness and fluidity in the hands and wrists. The dancers moved on to exercises to limber the back for working in Bukharan style, consisting of back bends performed both standing and kneeling.

Once the warm-up section of the class was completed, students learned choreographed dances in the various regional styles. In a second-year class I filmed, the students worked on three dances. The first was in the lyrical Farghana style, while the second was more like one in Bukharan style. The third seemed to incorporate movement motifs from all of the styles, so I am not sure what, if any, regional style the dance represented.

Work on turns followed. The students performed turns in a series traveling across the room and turning many times in place, finishing in a balanced pose. For the traveling turns the dancers moved in single file diagonally across the floor. The students performed three variations on a *chaîné* turn (a continuous series of turns performed on the balls of the feet), traveling to the right or to the left. The teacher asked for a series of eight turns across the floor, one in Farghana style, the second in Tajik style, and the last in Khorezm style.

The last exercise was the *doira dars* (the "drum dance"), an exercise with extensive rhythmic variations and corresponding movements. A teacher at the school told me that Tamara Khonim and Yusuf Kizikjon developed the *doira dars*, probably in the 1930s. The exercise taught students one movement (*harakat*) motif corresponding to each of the rhythmic patterns used in Uzbek classical music. By 1994, there were five variations of the *doira dars*, one for each year of the syllabus. The version I taped was for second-year students; there were increasingly difficult variations for each year up to the fifth year.

The *doira dars* for second-year students incorporated over fifteen different rhythmic patterns. For each pattern, students learned a corresponding movement motif. They performed some of the motifs staying in one place, then turning or traveling across the room. The dancers faces were intent as they followed the complex, asymmetrical rhythmic changes and meshed them with smooth changes from one set of movements to the next.

An example will illustrate the subtlety of the *doira dars* exercises. The rhythmic pattern was fast and asymmetrical like a running heartbeat:

The dancers first stood with their feet together and arms folded horizontally across their chests. Palms were flat facing the floor, and the fingertips of each hand touched the opposite forearm near the elbow. They moved just their heads from side to side in tiny, sinuous movements like a snake. Their heads stilled and their folded arms jutted from side to side in time to the shimmering pulse. Then the dancers began to tap the toes of their right feet along with their rocking arms. Pivoting on the left leg, the dancers began to turn a bit to the right with each tap of the right foot, slowly gliding into a turn, seemingly propelled by their folded arms.

A class I watched for the oldest students dispensed with the warm-up altogether. The students moved directly into working on choreographed dances. One girl wearing a gold embroidered cap (*döppi*) and braids past her waist performed *"Tanovar"* as a solo while the other six students watched her and sketched out the movements from the sides of the studio. The teacher called out dances by name one after the other and the students performed them. As they began each dance, my hostess, another teacher in the school, leaned over and told me the regional style of each dance. The students did dances from the Farghana, Khorezm, Tajik, and Bukharan regional styles.

DANCE TRAINING AS RITUAL

Becoming a dancer, then, entailed completing the prescribed program of study. The national dancers were the product of a process of a program of training and exercises. How did the dance training change the girls and boys who received it? How was dance education a tool for instilling a national consciousness in potential dancers? Catherine Bell (1992: 98) sees ritual practices as "a strategic form of socialization." Most helpful for our discussion is her view that ritual instills cultural awareness in participants' bodies:

The implicit dynamic and "end" of ritualization—that which it does not see itself doing—can be said to be the production of a "ritualized body." A ritualized body is a body invested with a "sense" of ritual. This sense of ritual exists as an implicit variety of schemes whose deployment works to produce sociocultural situations that the ritualized body can dominate in some way. This is a "practical mastery," to use Bourdieu's term, of strategic schemes for ritualization and it appears as a social instinct for creating and manipulating contrasts. This "sense" is not a matter of self-conscious knowledge of any explicit rules of ritual but is an implicit "cultivated disposition." (1992: 98, citing Bourdieu 1977: 1–4)

Viewing dance training as a strategy of socialization raises two sets of related questions about the body, ritual, and ways of knowing. One is the issue whether the principles embedded in ritual are culturally constructed or sociobiological. A second is whether and how ritual serves to instill and legitimize cultural understanding in and through the body. For example, Robert Hertz ([1909] 1973) argued that preferences for the right over the left hand corresponded to dualistic religious beliefs and visions of the cosmos.[6] Although historically rooted in clan and kinship groupings, the taxonomy embedded in the dance curriculum was a cultural construction. As discussed in Chapter 2, the "Uzbek" people as an ethnic group did not appear in historical records until the fourteenth century. The Soviets introduced the concept of nationhood and created the SSR of Uzbekistan in 1924 when they imposed national delimitation on their Central Asian territories. The formation of the Uzbek nation from historically disparate regions and peoples has already been established (see, e.g., Bauldauf 1991; Bacon [1966] 1980: 215–217; Allworth 1994: 256–259).

Turning to the second question, what is intriguing here is how "Uzbek" came to be accepted as a "natural" basis of collective identity despite its strained antecedents. Pierre Bourdieu ([1977] 1995: 78–87) asked how ideas, beliefs, and practices could become so accepted that they seem "automatic and impersonal." He said that a dialectic between the body and coded space instilled practical understanding:

But it is in the dialectical relationship between the body and a space structured according to the mythico-ritual oppositions that one finds the form par excellence of the structural apprenticeship which leads to the embodying of the structures of the world, that is, the appropriating by the world of a body thus enabled to appropriate the world. ([1977] 1995: 89)

The social awareness incorporated in space was a "generative schema," which Bourdieu defined in structuralist terms as pairs of oppositions such as high::low, light::shade and male::female ([1977] 1995: 89–90; see also Bell 1992: 98–104). Rather than looking at generating pairs of orienting concepts inculcated through dance classes, I look instead at a cultural taxonomy of dances taught at the *maktab*.

A "semantic domain" as defined by Charles Frake (1964) is helpful in mapping ethnic identities marked through dance in Uzbekistan. Frake said a semantic domain was "a set of related concepts" and that finding out concepts that people consider to be in the same domain and eliciting interlinkages across domains can reveal a people's "conceptual structure" (1964: 141). For example, Frake examined "interlinkages among the categories 'spice,' 'yeast,' 'beer' and 'drink' " (1964: 135–140). Adapting the same notion to dance, I would like to coin the notion of "kinetic domains" to discuss dances performed in Uzbekistan.

I argue that just as Frake identified "semantic domains," the curriculum at the *maktab* designated "kinetic domains." Furthermore, these kinetic domains corresponded to a geographic map of ethnic identities within Uzbekistan, and Uzbeks as a Soviet people. Viewing classes as rituals of socialization, I explore how teachers constructed and instilled an "Uzbek" national identity in students at the *maktab*. I will also briefly address socialization in two other areas: ideals of masculinity and femininity, and cohort formation.

What Is "Uzbek"?

Applying Charles Frake's approach, the curriculum used in the choreographic school set forth a cultural map of dance. The students were primarily expected to develop competence in the three regional styles of Farghana, Bukhara, and Khorezm. These three styles constituted "Uzbek" national dances. The Uzbek "national" identity, as represented in dance, was an amalgam of three historically significant centers of power and culture (see Chapter 2).

During the week of exams in the spring, I had the privilege of seeing the examinations of seventeen classes. I attended six sessions of three to five examinations over the period of a month. This experience afforded me a compact overview of the five-year training curriculum. I saw examinations of classes for the following levels:

	Total classes	Girls	Boys
First year	1 class	1	
Second year	4 classes	3	1*
Third year	1 class	1	
Fourth year	4 classes	3*	1*
Fifth year	6 classes	4	2

Note: *I did not hear anyone mention the level of three of the examinations I saw. Using the age of the students and the dances they performed, I have estimated their level.

Each group demonstrated three to five dances for the committee. The first- and second-year students covered the same material they studied in the class description above: positions of the arms, exercises to develop suppleness in the wrists and arms, back bends, and the *doira dars*. One to three dances in the Farghana style showing basic movement vocabulary as well as turns completed the lower-level exams.

Fourth- and fifth-year students had to show proficiency in Farghana, Khorezm, and Bukharan styles of dance. The first examination I saw was for a class of ten teenage girls in the fifth level (*kurs*). They all wore royal blue leotards, pink tights, black knee-length skirts, and heeled shoes. After bowing to the committee and to the musicians, the group performed a *doira dars*. They demonstrated three more dances. The first was to music in a ¾ meter and was in the lyrical Farghana style. For the second dance, in Khorezm style, they wore bells on their wrists, jingling them as they moved their arms through *holat*. The third piece demonstrated their command of Bukharan technique, featuring sharp movements of the shoulders and back bends. They finished with turns across the room in the Farghana and Bukharan styles and a third set of turns in a style I did not recognize.

There were often murmurs among the panel about whether a group as a whole was performing up to the appropriate level for students in their year of study. One group performed only two pieces, and forgot sections of the dances they attempted. One of the panelists sharply rebuked the class for their poor performance and slow progress. The students' instructor also became quite flushed and uncomfortable. Mastery of dances in each of the major regional styles seemed to be a significant criterion of progress and excellence.

At the end of the morning's testing, the students left. Behind closed doors, the teachers discussed what grades students should receive. I was allowed to overhear the discussion only one time because a teacher observed me making notes on the discussion, so I was not invited to listen in on the other evaluations. Students received a grade ranging from a low of one to a high of five for their performance. Whether the students were Uzbek or Russian was also discussed. Although I could not follow the entire conversation, it appeared that being of Uzbek origin was advantageous.

Just as the narratives of the dancers were cast in the form of an itinerary through places and institutions (see Chapter 2), the classes for professional dancers can be seen as kinetic and visual tours of Uzbekistan. The three regional styles of movement were grouped under the unifying classification of "Uzbek" dance, corresponding to the way the three historically distinct geographic regions of Farghana, Bukhara, and Khorezm had been welded together by the Soviet national delimitation that occurred in 1924 (see Chapter 2).

I asked Dilorum what could be learned from looking at Uzbek dances. She responded:

Well, there are many kinds of dance. For example, the *shtat* [literally, "state," perhaps she meant province?] of Khorezm, the *shtat* of Andijon, the *shtat* of Tashkent. There they also have all kinds of music, their own music, their own approach. That is to say, for example, the people of Khorezm and of Farghana are not the same kind [switching to English] another dance. . . . Each has its own movement. There are many kinds of movements. There are many kinds of classical songs [*maqom*]. Andijon's is different. Khorezm's is different. For example in Bukhara—the emir of Bukhara—[dance] is influenced by Tajiks in ancient times. For example, in Russia, French was necessary. [Switching to French] You speak French [*Parlez vous francais*]. . . . In Samarkand, Farsi [Persian].

In addition to the dances designated as "Uzbek," the students learned other kinds of dance. Examining Uzbek dance as a category of dance in relation to other categories of dance reveals how the identity "Uzbek" is positioned in relation to other groups. During their training at the school, children studied dances attributed to other Soviet Central Asian nationalities such as Uyghur and Karakalpok, two minority groups in the republic of Uzbekistan.

The school also offered classes in "classical" dance. "Classical" dance was Russian ballet, and people even referred to it using the Russian terms *klassiksii tanz* or *ballet*; no Uzbek word existed for this dance form. All of the students at the school studied ballet and Uzbek dance. Some of the students specialized in Uzbek dance, while others specialized in ballet. Uzbekistan had one major classical ballet company, the Alisher Navoi Opera and Ballet Theater. The Navoi company ranks included many graduates of the ballet program at the choreographic school.

A few of the older dancers, such as Dilorum, occasionally mentioned learning or teaching "international" dances. I saw it only once in Uzbekistan at a performance by students of the choreographic school. Two students performed a dance intended to be a Spanish Flamenco dance. The young girl wore a swirling red ruffled skirt and her male partner wore a white full shirt, black boots, and tights. They stamped their heels and arched their backs while looking at each other flirtatiously.

A conceptual mapping of dance forms taught at the choreographic school can therefore be summarized as follows:

National (*millii*) Dances	Classic (*klassikskii*) Dances	"National" (*narodnii*) Dances
Farghana dance	Ballet	Spanish
Bukharan dance Uzbek dance	Uyghur	Other?
Khorenzm dance	Karakalpok	

Turning to dance, the *millii* dances include both dances from different regions in Uzbekistan, such as Farghana and Bukhara, and from different ethnic groups such as Uyghur and Karakalpok. Ethnic identity and regional identity are not, however, unrelated categories. The Karakalpoks live principally in a region near the Aral Sea within the Uzbek borders, while the Uyghurs are an Uzbek-speaking ethnic group in Sinkiang Province in China. Bukhara, as Dilorum explained above, is historically associated with Tajik (Persian) influence. Moreover, all of the ethnic groups represented in the category of *millii* dance at the *maktab* are Uzbek-speaking peoples. Thus blood, geography, and language establish "inter-linkages," to use Frake's (1964: 134) term, among the concepts Farghana, Bukhara, Khorezm, Uyghur, Karakalpok, Uzbek, and *millii*.

It is important to note that outside the walls of the school, the term "*millii*" referred to a broad range of ethnic groups. "Japanese" was an appropriate response when I was asked, "*Millatese nima?*" ("What is your nationality?")[7] Similarly, an Uzbek to Uzbek dictionary given to me by an Uzbek language scholar defined *millat* as:

A group of people which is historically formed and which comes together on the common basis of the spiritual distinctiveness of culture, language, territory, and economic life. Russian nationality, Uzbek nationality. . . . Kazak, Kirgiz, Armenian and Jewish. (Ma'rufov 1981: 464)

I think that the narrower meaning of *millii* at the *maktab* reflected the fact that the school did not teach dances of all of the populations in Uzbekistan. I also think that the designation "*millii*" in the context of the dance school marked a basic dichotomy between Russian ballet and other dances of non-Russian peoples.

Although *narodnii* means "nation" in Russian, I heard dancers use the term primarily for dances of peoples outside the Soviet Union. Looking at the categories for dance, a second subset of terms thus consists of *"Mil-lii," "Narodnii,"* and *"Klassikskii."* Dancers used the terms *"klassikskii"* and *"ballet"* interchangeably, but rarely noted that ballet was Russian. "Russian" was thus an unmarked category. I suspect that this tripartite mapping corresponds to a construction of Uzbekistan's place in the Soviet political order. *"Millii"* designated Uzbekistan's status as one of the Soviet Union's subject peoples. The unmarked status of ballet as a Russian art corresponded to Russia's supremacy as a colonial power. *"Narodnii"* mapped the rest of the globe outside of the Soviet Union.

Students learned different movement vocabularies corresponding to different ethnic groupings. To use Catherine Bell's terms, training invested their bodies with a "practical mastery" of the kinetic domains constituting both "Uzbek" dances and "dances in Uzbekistan." The kinetic domains, in turn, corresponded to a political and geographic ordering of Uzbekistan, Russia, and peoples outside the Soviet Union. As they learned to dance, students thereby absorbed a conceptual map of Uzbekistan, the Soviet Union, and the world.

With independence, however, the ordering set out in a taxonomy of terms for kinds of dance appeared to be changing. In 1992 when I met a ballet dancer who performed with the Navoi Opera and Ballet Theater in Tashkent, I told her I was interested in *özbek raqsi* (Uzbek dance). She immediately asked, *"Özbek raqslari yoki raqslar Özbekistanda?"* (Uzbek dances or dances *in* Uzbekistan?).

Ballet was not an Uzbek dance even when performed in Uzbekistan by Uzbeks. The distinction between an Uzbek and Russian identity was clearly marked in classes at the *maktab.* I observed a class of second-year Uzbek dance students in 1994 when the teacher corrected the way the students were standing. They were standing with the weight evenly balanced between both feet, heads up, and backs straight. The teacher shook her head. She eased her weight onto one leg, settling into her hip with a relaxed spine (imagine a hitchhiker who is not holding out her thumb). "This," she said, standing like a soldier at attention, "is Russian." Easing into the hitchhiker stance she continued, "This is Uzbek."

What is perhaps most significant about the mapping is that it corresponds to a subtle distinction I heard people make between *özbek* and *özbekistonlik.* An Uzbek anthropologist explained the difference to me. *"Özbek,"* referring to Uzbek ethnic descent, is an ascribed status, but *"özbek-istonlik"* denotes citizenship in the republic of Uzbekistan and can be acquired.

The distinction arose again while discussing the Uzbek tradition of hospitality. One young graduate student of Uzbek descent, Jamila, explained *özbek* in primordial terms, as a capacity for kindness that could only come from Uzbek blood:

Jamila: Other groups—

MD: Like Koreans?

Jamila: —could not be *özbek*, they could be *özbekistonlik*.

MD: Why?

Jamila: Some things, in the blood, they could never be so generous.

MD: But what is in this box of *özbekistonlik*?

Jamila [looks down, thinks]: For example, my father is very kind and generous; I am very proud of him. There was a family next door to us. They had eight children and the father left them to live with another wife. The wife was a little bit [finger to temple, twisting]. They did not have enough food. We were not rich, just okay, but my father helped them. We had a donkey so my father could bring flour for us and for them. The mother-in-law used to come every night and bless us.

The emphasis on "Uzbek dances" as opposed to "dances in Uzbekistan" reflects a new consciousness among dancers and nondancers of the distinction between *özbek* as an ethnic marker, and *özbekistonlik*, as the jural status of a citizen of the republic of Uzbekistan.

Gender

Although there are few professional male dancers in Uzbekistan, I also observed examinations of four classes of boys. The boys wore sleeveless white T-shirts and black pants gathered at the ankle. The boys did not do *holat* or series of turns across the room. Instead, they did a *doira dars* and energetic dances emphasizing speed, strength, and agility. Unlike the girls who swayed delicately on the balls of their feet and moved their arms in gentle curves, the boys stood tall, stomped their feet with resounding thumps, slashed the air with arms like blades, jumped high in the air, or spun quickly into a drop to one knee.

I asked one highly regarded teacher what qualities male and female dancers should have. The teacher said men should be *shokh* and *qattiq*. "*Shokh*" is a term that roughly translates as aggressive, strong, and uncontrolled. A desirable trait in males, but a fault in females. While visiting a family, I heard a paternal grandmother scold a little girl for running around the dining room or tussling with her cousin while we were eating. She screamed at the toddler and called her a *shaytan* (devil). Her harshness was unusual; on every other occasion I can recall, Uzbeks were patient, affectionate, and indulgent with small children.

Several weeks later I complimented the grandmother on how intelligent her granddaughter was. She told me with a frown and a pinched mouth that her granddaughter was *shokh*. The child was bright, insisted on being the center of attention, and strong-willed. The child's maternal grandmother told me with a rueful smile that she had given the child a piece of candy. The child immediately reached for another piece, saying, "That's mine too." *"Shokh"* was thus a troubling quality in girls.

"Qattiq" literally means "hard." In the context of dance, it seemed to mean forceful, direct, bound movement. When dance teachers used the word, they would clench their fists and make a short dropping movement as though pounding something to emphasize what they meant by *qattiq.*

Curiously, three Uzbek women used *qattiq* with a clenched fist to describe what kind of husbands Uzbek men made. To illustrate, one young single friend was discussing the plight of new brides in Tashkent (as opposed to brides in other regions of Uzbekistan). She said that they were seldom allowed to go out and labored long hours doing all of the domestic work for the husband's family. If the brides managed to stay in school, they were often so tired they fell asleep in class. As she explained that Tashkentese husbands were known for being domineering and inconsiderate, she squeezed her fist and said that the men were *qattiq.*

Age Sets

The third and final schema is grouping by age. Age sets are a form of stratification familiar to anthropologists (see, e.g., Evans-Pritchard [1940] 1969: 249–261). I address them briefly because the choreographic school system contributed to forming the cohorts that are a fundamental aspect of the social organization of Uzbek dance. As discussed earlier in this chapter, students progressed through five levels in the course of their training. I visited the school repeatedly over ten months in 1994 and saw that classes of students remained together throughout the year. For the exams each member of a group wore the same combination of leotards, skirts, and tights.

I became acquainted with the oldest group of students and was able to follow their paths from graduation in the spring of 1994 through joining professional companies. Three or four students from the oldest class were parceled out as apprentices to each of the major companies throughout the spring. They joined the companies full time in August. I noticed that the recent graduates tended to cluster together as newcomers during rehearsal breaks. At least for the first year of their new jobs, the age sets formed at the choreographic school continued.

In one company I visited in 1992, the five newest company members had a dressing room separate from the more senior dancers. They told me that they had come to the same choreographic school when they were ten and had lived and studied there until they joined the company. When I returned in 1994, all but one of the new dancers had left. The remaining dancer had moved into a more senior position of unofficial leadership among her colleagues and chatted with many of them.

I suspect that as dancers progressed beyond graduation, the ties to their

graduating class weakened, but status as an alumna of a particular choreographic school in Tashkent continued to be important. Many I met
attended the same choreographic school in Tashkent. I met one dancer
who had attended a different choreographic school in Bukhara but suc-
ceeded in winning a place in a Tashkent company. She usually strolled
alone in hallways or the studio during breaks while the other dancers
flocked together, shared snacks, and chatted. Although she appeared to
possess technical training equal to that of her colleagues, she was excluded
from their informal social networks.

CONCLUSION

By the 1940s extensive training was essential to becoming a dancer. In
Dilorum's words the dancers considered themselves "professionals." This
is not to say that the dancers beginning their careers in the 1930s did not
receive training. Roziya Karimova's life history (see Chapter 2) shows that
she studied dance in school and received special training from Tamara
Khonim and Kari Yakubov after they recruited her to dance. Exercises
created then, such as the *doira dars*, were still an important part of the
curriculum in 1994. What is significant, however, is the way that dancers
spoke about criteria for becoming dancers. Mukarram Turghunbayeva
spoke of "heart" and "coordination." Dilorum, on the other hand, stressed
formal education as well as talent.

By 1994, dance training was a ritual, inculcating a practical sense of
fundamental principles of social ordering. The classes the children at the
maktab took instilled a conceptual map corresponding to the political and
geographic configuration of the Uzbek republic, Russia as the dominant
focus of the Soviet empire, the collective membership of nationalities
within the Soviet Union, and of the Soviet people among other peoples
of the world.

Each dance class was a symbolic journey through the territory of Uzbek-
speaking peoples—Farghana, Bukhara, and Khorezm—with occasional
forays to the Karakalpokistan and the Uyghurs in Sinkiang Province. The
curriculum as a whole was a guided tour of Russia, "Uzbek" nationalities,
and peoples of Europe. By the completion of the five-year curriculum, the
students' bodies were "acculturated" with mastery of multiple kinetic domains representing many peoples. Dance also instilled at least two other
fundamental social schema: norms for male and female dancing, and an
enduring sense of identity with a cohort.

NOTES

1. Russian and European ballet, however, had always featured patterned and
synchronized groups of dancers. In America extravaganzas like Busby Berkeley

musicals became popular in the late 1930s and 1940s. Perhaps these dances registered America's transition to an industrial society, where new material technologies produced identical items, and new managerial methods coordinated the labor of multitudes of factory workers.

2. I have notated the time line using the TUBS (Time Unit Box System), which allocates one box per beat. The TUBS has the advantage of illustrating rhythmic patterns without relying on the European musical system of meters such as ¾ or ¼. Musicians usually played without written music, so I do not have sufficient data at this time to know whether the European time signatures would be appropriate.

I have marked heavily accented beats with an "x" and more lightly accented beats with a "*." The *doira* (drum) player establishes the time line for the other musicians. Players produce a wide variety of timbres by striking closer or farther from the rim of the *doira*, altering the shape of their hands or even rippling their fingers on the rim. I have not tried to indicate the timbres because there are many.

3. The dates of her tours covered a fifteen-year period. In summarizing her touring and performing, however, she says that she toured with pan-Soviet companies for twenty-five years.

4. A "club" was an auditorium on a collective farm (*kolkhoz*) where movies were shown and concerts were held. The hall was also used for social activities such as playing cards.

5. Dilorum was referring to the Alisher Navoi Opera and Ballet Theater in Tashkent. The theater had a proscenium stage, high ceilings, and seats for hundreds of people. I counted some fifty people at a concert I attended; they did not even fill a handful of rows in the center section.

6. Hertz asked, "How could man's body, the microcosm, escape the law of polarity which governs everything? . . . If human asymmetry had not existed, it would have had to be invented" ([1909] 1973: 10).

7. *Millat* is a noun meaning "nationality," while *millii* is the adjective from the same root and can be translated as "national."

4

From Genealogical to Generic (circa 1954–1990)

CORE AND PERIPHERY

Chapter 3 traced the institutionalization of Uzbek dance and a bifurcation between the "national" dances performed on stage by professional dancers and the "folkoric" dances people did at social events such as weddings. Dilorum's comment, "We made Uzbek dance into a beautiful diamond," invited me to view Uzbek national dances as commodities that were produced and refined under Soviet auspice. In this chapter, "From Genealogical to Generic,"[1] I view Uzbek dance as a commodity produced during the Soviet periods.

I argue that the institutional development of Uzbek dance parallels the development of material resources during the Soviet period. I focus on the time period from the 1950s through the 1980s. The patterns I identify in this chapter began as early as 1919 but became more defined during the years from the 1950s through the 1980s. I also choose these decades because they were the active years of a cohort of artists who received training after World War II.

In terms of structure, the institutional framework for producing national dances followed the paradigm of core and periphery (Frank 1966; Campbell 1991) established for the development of material resources. Although Andre Gunder Frank's research focused on the impact of capitalism on global development, his model of core and periphery helps to clarify the organization of dance in the Soviet colonial empire.

Frank (1979; 1966) asked why the capitalist system led to development in some regions and underdevelopment in others. He identified a pattern of relationships that pervaded colonial Latin America. He explained that "contemporary underdevelopment is in large part the historical product of past and continuing economic and other relations between the satellite underdeveloped and the now developed metropolitan countries" (1966:

18). Urban areas became commercial centers that siphoned surplus capital from outlying areas into the hub. The national and colonial capitals, in turn, became satellites supplying the world economic system (1966: 20).

Although Frank described the model of core and periphery in the context of capitalist economic systems, the model is equally apposite for characterizing local, regional, national, and unionwide relationships in the Soviet empire. Robert Campbell (1991: 10) likened the Soviet centrally planned economy to a "single corporation in charge of all production in the society: 'USSR, Inc.' " The government tells enterprises how much to produce and is the sole supplier of goods and the sole purchaser of labor. The state is also the sole mediator between the domestic economy and world markets (1991: 11).[2]

The Soviets implemented the command economy to develop natural resources in Uzbekistan (Rumer 1989). For example, the highly fertile land in Uzbekistan was devoted to cotton monoculture, and the raw cotton was exported to other republics for processing into cloth. The finished product eventually arrived in Moscow, for use in Russia or for sale abroad. Like cotton, Uzbek dances were resources that were produced, refined, and exported during the Soviet period.

CENTRALIZED PRODUCTION OF UZBEK DANCES

Connections between the national metropolis of Tashkent and Russia began even during the Bolshevik years. The Central Asian poet, dancer, and musician Zokirjon Holmuhammad o'g'li, better known as Furqat, went to St. Petersburg in 1919 to perform Uzbek songs and dances. Tamara Khonim studied dance in Moscow (Swift 1968: 181) as did Mukarram Turghunbayeva (Avdeyeva 1989). During World War II promising dance students were sent to Moscow for training. Uzbek artists also competed in festivals held in Moscow. One dancer I met won medals for her dancing in a youth festival held in Russia after the war.

Dancers from Uzbekistan continued to receive training in Moscow during the 1950s and the decades that followed. I attended a performance of a ballet company in Tashkent. Friends told me that one of the company's principal dancers had been trained in Moscow. I also met several Uzbek national dancers who had studied in Moscow.

In 1994 dancers spoke of individuals who had studied in Moscow with great respect. I gathered only partial career histories of individuals who began their careers in the 1950s because they were extremely busy individuals who had become the leading directors, teachers, and choreographers of Uzbek professional dance. Most of my data about this group consists of observing them at work and from brief discussions during rehearsals or class breaks about the works in progress.

To my knowledge, every prominent teacher or choreographer I met in

1994 graduated from a choreographic school. Upon graduation they performed with one of the national dance companies in Tashkent. Some had
studied ballet and possibly character dance for extended periods in Moscow or toured with pan-Soviet companies. Dance education thus centered
on the Soviet hub in Moscow. Dancers trained in Moscow returned to
Uzbekistan and became leading performers, choreographers, and teachers.

Within Uzbekistan, the capital city of Tashkent functioned as a regional
hub for dance. Children from all over Uzbekistan came to Tashkent to
study at a choreographic school. Some graduates of the school made their
careers with one of the national dance companies in Tashkent. Others
worked with regional dance companies. I met the director of a regional
company who worked in a provincial *madaniyat yurt* (house of culture).
In her late thirties, she had studied at the choreographic school in Tashkent and danced with one of the national companies in Tashkent for
several years. She had come back then to her native city to teach and
direct a company.

The company consisted of about twelve teenage girls. The dances they
rehearsed showed the influence of Tashkent training and choreography
on dance in the provinces. For example, the company rehearsed a dance
called the "Andijon Polka." I had seen another version of the "Andijon
Polka" in classes at the choreographic school in Tashkent. Although Andijon was a region famous for a distinctively slow, weighty dance style, the
"Andijon Polka" was not based on indigenous dances. It was a quick, buoy-
ant new work created by professional dancers and musicians. Thus the
"Andijon Polka" was a work that disseminated from the national dance
schools to the provinces. Perpetuating the cycle of exchange between the
core and periphery, one young girl in the group was going to Tashkent
in the fall to study at the choreographic school.

MOSCOW TRAINING

According to Mary Grace Swift (1968: 214–218) choreographic schools
in Moscow and Leningrad became means of disseminating ballet training
to satellite countries. Two of the most famous schools were the Vaganova
Choreographic Institute, associated with the Kirov Theater in Leningrad,
and the Moscow Choreographic Institute, affiliated with the Bolshoi Theater. A few individuals from regions outside of Russia studied in Leningrad
as early as 1905 (Anya Peterson Royce, personal communication). In 1946
the Soviet government began recruiting students from outside of Russia
for choreographic training.

Training dance actors to portray Soviet themes was a central concern
of dance educators (Swift 1968: 214). In 1934 a pedagogical department
was formed in Leningrad to encourage dance teachers and students to

use political themes in their work. In 1938 a conference was held in Moscow to discuss unified training to teach dancers to depict Soviet heroes. In 1950 the Moscow Choreographic Institute added a course on "Studies on Contemporary Themes." At a conference of leading Russian artistic directors and dance educators, the speakers stated: "The Soviet ballet school attempts to arm the young ballet generation by means of new, clear, mighty and expressive choreographic speech, to answer to the tasks of socialist realism in ballet" (1968: 214, citing A. Belosel'skii, *"Molodye Kadry Baleta," Teatr,* no. 9 [1950]: 87). According to Matvei Gorbunov (1960: 67–68, cited in Swift 1968: 216) in 1960 the Lunacharsky State Institute of Theatrical Art (GITIS) in Moscow trained ballet masters, actors, directors, and arts scholars. The Lunacharsky Institute designed curricula and teaching materials for other theatrical schools, and offered them for discussion at annual conferences convened by the Ministry of Culture of the USSR. Postgraduate offerings included courses in Marxist–Leninist esthetics.

Dancers I interviewed did not discuss the ideological aspects of their training with me. I asked several dancers active during the 1950s and 1960s about the dances they used to perform or about the kinds of themes addressed. I usually got a shrug or a response on a different topic, which may have been a function of my limited ability to ask complex questions in the Uzbek language. One dancer briefly mentioned a dance she did with a series of turns that always brought vigorous applause from the audience. Another told me about a teacher who had studied in Moscow. He spoke only about how very knowledgeable and strong the teacher was. Although political themes were important from the perspective of Soviet policy, the dancers seemed more concerned with artistic issues, such as technical virtuosity and communicating with their audiences.

One dancer, Dilbar, discussed her Moscow training with me. She said she had been trained as a *"ballet mester."* I did not fully understand what this meant until she taught me a dance. She chose a dance that began with slow, sensual motifs accelerating into a series of turns and ending with quick, sparkling side steps and a ripple of notes plucked on the *dutar* (long-necked, string instrument). I was quite uncomfortable with the co-quettish quality of the beginning of the dance. She explained the dancer's entrance and character, saying: "Do not be afraid, you are the most beautiful dancer in the city." Some of the motifs seemed quite suggestive to me, such as drawing a hand across the chest and undulating the shoulders. She assured me that they indicated friendship rather than seduction.

Nevertheless, I continued to wish myself at the bottom of the ocean each time we started the dance. After becoming quite exasperated with me, she asked what was wrong. I told her that my mother was pretty, but I was not, so I did not feel right doing the dance. She looked at me fiercely and said that whenever I do this dance, I must tell myself: "Dilbar is my teacher." She proceeded to demonstrate the steps with panache. I took a deep breath, thought of the many famous dancers whose footsteps permeated the very carpet I stood on, and did the dance again with all the energy and assurance I could muster. The dance came alive, and the turns and quick steps unfurled easily from the deadly beginning. She urged me to pour more and more energy into the movements as the tempo accelerated to a sprightly finish.

We discussed the dance later. She said that she had thought and felt that particular dance was right for me. She said, when I had first started doing the dance she taught, "You seemed so . . . ," and she pulled a long face to show that I had been lifeless. But her instincts had been confirmed when I finally found the essence of the dance. She knew the dance had been what I needed.

My own modern dance training in America had emphasized speed, strength, and energy. The gentle movements of Uzbek dance felt somewhat empty to me. Although she had never seen me dance and only chatted with me a few times, Dilbar had somehow sensed that I had not found a way to channel my own spirit into Uzbek dance. The dance she taught me was a happy compromise between my athletic instincts and the more restrained forms of Uzbek dance. Pleased with my thanks, she said, "I am a ballet master." Her training had shown her how to bring out each dancer's unique qualities. I understood why she was one of the most respected choreographers in Uzbekistan.

This episode also suggested some of the differences in concepts of selfhood and femininity between dancers and nondancers. I felt very constrained during my first months in Uzbekistan and finally realized my discomfort was due to the stillness of Uzbek women. They sat firmly on their chairs, feet crossed at the ankles. They punctuated conversation with their voices but not their hands. One older woman I know always chided me when I zipped into a room or set a teacup down too hard. "Gently," she would say, "don't rush." Younger women deferred to older women. For example, younger women often listened while older women spoke but made few, if any, comments. By the time I began working with Dilbar, I had learned to minimize movements and facial expressions to avoid drawing undue attention on the street or in gatherings. The bold individuality Dilbar encouraged me to find and express felt uncomfortably flamboyant after so many months of striving for innocuous invisibility.

THE *USTA* SYSTEM AS FICTIVE KINSHIP

The colonial structure of core and periphery, however, did not function as a monolith. How did individuals function within the Soviet system? Scholars such as Michael Rywkin (1990) have speculated that one of the strategies some Central Asian peoples used to resist Soviet reforms was to

maintain indigenous extended family relationships within new Soviet institutions. For example, in Kazakstan nomadic tribes were forcibly settled
on *kolkhozes* (collective farms). Extended kin groups, however, continued
to function as an economic and social unit within the Soviet structure of
collective farms (Bacon [1966] 1980: 135–137).

The life and career histories I elicited from dancers provide a glimpse
of a model that resembled the more intimate dynamics of kinship embedded within the colonial and national institutions. When I elicited life
histories, dancers would frequently mention their *usta.* The term *"usta"*
can be roughly translated as "master." I heard the word used in several
ways. It was used in general conversation to indicate skill in a particular
arena. One mother used the word to praise her daughter's domestic accomplishments. She said the young woman was an *usta* in baking, and
proceeded to tell me about the layered Napoleon pastry her child could
make. I also heard graduate students call their faculty adviser an *usta.*

In the context of dance, professional dancers used the term to refer to
their principal teacher. The relationship between a dancer and her *usta*
is rich and lasts throughout a dancer's career. For example, when I began
to ask about dances performed during the 1940s by Mukarram Turghunbayeva, one of the early Uzbek dancers, professional dancers told me to
look at the work of Mamura Ergasheva, a dancer who had been Turghunbayeva's star pupil. In addition to teaching, I also observed *ustas* creating
choreography for their protégés and helping them to obtain employment.
Even retired dancers would tell me who their *usta* was.

Dancers had only one *usta,* although they may have studied with many
teachers in the course of their training. Every famous and successful dancer I interviewed had an *usta.* Not all dancers mentioned having an *usta,*
however. One dancer who was not well-known explained that no one had
taken a particular interest in her career and helped her.

An *usta,* in turn, referred to a protégé as a *"shogurd"* (apprentice). My
own experiences indicate that an *usta* works with a *shogurd* privately, outside of group classes. As I describe in Chapter 2 and earlier in this chapter,
the two *ustas* I worked with had me learn set pieces of choreography and
taught me technique, movement, vocabulary, and interpretation through
refining and correcting my performances of the choreographed dances.
I received far more detailed assistance and critiques than students in
group classes at the choreographic *maktab.*

The relationship between an *usta* and a *shogurd* can be warmly personal.
I attended several social events where a former student visited her *usta*
for tea, bringing a gift or a home-baked cake to show respect. One dancer's husband-to-be asked her *usta* as well as her family for approval of
the marriage. If an *usta* introduced me to her protégés, the protégés were
usually helpful to me thereafter. When I began studying Uzbek dance with
a teacher, Uzbek friends referred to her as my *usta.* In addition

to teaching me dance, my *usta* fed me, called me her daughter, corrected my Uzbek, and made me a tonic when she thought I looked anemic.

Three major "lineages" of dance *ustas* emerged during my research. Two started with the early Uzbek dancers Tamara Khonim and Mukarram Turghunbayeva. The third originated in Bukhara. The Bukharan dancer most frequently identified as an *usta* by the dancers I met in Tashkent was Isahar Akilov, a dancer and choreographer who rose to prominence during the 1930s. Senior or retired dancers generally gave me one of these three names when they identified their *ustas*. Dancers who appeared to be about age thirty or younger had an *usta* trained by one of these three teachers.

Thus, within the Soviet structure of core and periphery, Uzbek dancers created strong personal ties. The relationship between a dancer and an *usta* is like the relationship between a child and a parent, with lifelong guidance and mutual support. Most prominent dancers are professional descendants of one of three early Uzbek dancers; therefore, the bonds of fictive kinship spanned three generations of dancers. Within the very institutions created to break up Central Asian family structures, Uzbek dancers formed new fictive kinship relationships.[3]

Mentoring relationships are not unusual in the field of dance. Ballet history, for example, is rich in famous Pygmalions such as Sergey Pavlovich Diaghilev (1872–1929) and George Balanchine (1904–1983). Nevertheless, I did find the kind of bonding that occurred between *ustas* and their students intriguing in the context of Central Asian culture. In my dealings with other women in household settings, I learned that the relationships between mothers and daughters are quite close and loving. With this exception, relationships between women tended to be highly competitive.

Through my own experiences and in speaking with Uzbek friends, I realized that the only paradigm for "adopting" a woman into a household was as a new bride. For example, the relationship between a bride and her mother-in-law was often fraught with tension. The new bride had the lowest status in the household and assumed the bulk of the housework. Her mother-in-law was responsible for teaching the bride her new duties. Some mothers-in-law were kind, but many treated their new daughters-in-law quite harshly. One young woman explained that mothers-in-law could be jealous of a bride's youth and beauty, and took advantage of their senior status to exploit the newcomer. Single women who stayed with relatives often found themselves responsible for the bulk of the household duties, like a new bride.

The cooperative relationships between *ustas* and their protégés was therefore more like the cooperative relationship between a mother and a daughter, than the asymmetrical relationship prevailing between an older woman and a new member of the household. Perhaps the fact that many of the earliest dancers were orphans made the ties between *ustas* and their students take the most intimate form usually reserved for blood relatives, rather than the instrumental and even oppressive dynamic that usually characterized ties through marriage or adoption.

The *usta* relationship was important in a number of fields besides dance. As mentioned above, I heard graduate students refer to their faculty advisers as *ustas*. I also met a family in which the son had been apprenticed to an *usta* to learn a traditional Central Asian art form. Although I did not have the opportunity to observe these relationships closely, instances like these suggest that the *usta* relationship occurs in both indigenous professions, such as Central Asian art, and fields, such as dance, created during the Soviet period.

DECENTRALIZED PRODUCTION OF SOCIAL DANCES

Production of social dances continued in decentralized private arenas such as weddings and cradle parties. However, even these events, were affected by Soviet rule. I talked to one woman in a rural area who appeared to be sixty or seventy years old. She said that people did not dance at her wedding, and the men and women had celebrated separately.

All of the weddings I attended in 1992 and 1994 were joint celebrations with men and women together. At least one band, and often two or three, played dance music for the guests. I asked when the ceremonies had changed, and I was told that the joint celebration was called a "Red Wedding." It was introduced during the Soviet period when the young Uzbeks wanted to celebrate in a more modern fashion. Christel Lane (1981: 62–63) notes that Red Weddings were first introduced as alternatives to Christian ceremonies in the 1920s and became accepted throughout the USSR by the late 1960s. Although Lane does not specify where Red Weddings first occurred, from the context of her discussion it seems that she may be referring to Moscow and Leningrad.

Social reproduction of dances occurred in households, at private social events, and in schools. Uzbek children learned to dance by playing with relatives and watching and participating at social events. While visiting Uzbek homes I saw women dandle babies in their laps and sing. They held the child's hands up above the shoulders, forearms bent ninety degrees at the elbows (like a bank teller's response when a robber says "Stick 'em up"), and, in time to the song, gently rotated the palms of the hands back and forth to face behind the child, then toward the front. At weddings, this arm and hand motif was one of the most common movements women and men performed.

Teenagers and children I met during 1992 and 1994 also learned to dance in school and from television. I visited one household for dinner. When the mother of the household learned that I was interested in dance, she persuaded her daughter, who appeared to be about eight years old, to dance for the guests. The little girl danced to taped music. She appeared to be improvising, but had a very extensive vocabulary of steps and hand motifs. She also punctuated the complex rhythms of the music with precisely timed gestures and pauses. She performed with polish and aplomb. Her mother said she learned to dance in school.

The influence of schooling and, as discussed below, of television may lead to diffusion of professional Uzbek dance motifs into social dancing within the next several decades. I did not ask when dance became part of the public school curriculum. I suspect dance was introduced into the public schools about twenty years ago. From observing dancers at weddings, women over about age twenty-five tended to have a relatively small vocabulary of movement motifs that they repeated over and over. Women and girls younger than about age twenty-five seemed to have larger movement vocabularies and use more rhythms in their dancing. These differences may reflect training in dance and musical training. They may also be a function of social expectations that matrons should move more calmly and sedately than younger women.

NATIONAL AND FOLKLORIC DANCE FORMS

Thus, the state national dance institutions did not displace or suppress the processes of production and reproduction of social dances. Two genres of Uzbek dance developed. The first, called "klassik raqs," refers to the dances performed by professional state dancers; and the second, "folklorik raqs," refers to dances performed by amateurs and nonprofessionals at social events.

After about six months of field research I attended a wedding. I saw a white-haired woman watching closely when I was dragged onto the dance floor. Although I had been studying Uzbek national dances for nearly six months, I found myself holding back, unsure what kinds of movements to do. I realized that the steps I had been learning in my formal Uzbek dance lessons were inappropriate in this social setting. They would have been too "showy"—traveling over too much space and the motifs too complex and crisply defined. I looked at women near me and tried to copy a few simple movements. The elderly woman watching assessed my efforts with a sniff of disdain.

Incidents like this one led me to question what, if any, was the relationship between indigenous dance forms and dances that became designated as "national" dances during the Soviet period? A comparative analysis of professional Uzbek dance technique and a folkloric dance suggests that three processes of transformation occurred: elaboration, nationalization, and standardization.

Elaboration

The national dances performed by professional dancers bear only a faint resemblance to social dances I saw at weddings and social occasions. I asked several noted professional dancers about the relationship between professional Uzbek dance technique and the kinds of folk dances people performed at social events such as weddings. They told me with pride that the dances professional dancers performed were quite different. One said to me that the social dances were simple and not very interesting. She demonstrated with a few shuffling steps and shrugged, with a sour face. She went on to explain that most of the professional dance vocabulary had been created by professional dancers.

Ballet was one of the major influences on the professional Uzbek dance vocabulary. Some dancers criticized balletic steps as inauthentic. On the other hand, one teacher who had studied in Moscow explained that ballet had been beneficial for Uzbek dance because it led to the development of Uzbek dance technique. The similarities between ballet and professional Uzbek dance techniques are marked. I observed an advanced dance class taught by a teacher who had studied in Moscow. The structure of the class and many of the exercises were the same as a ballet class.

A ballet class begins with exercises at the barre to strengthen and stretch the muscles, then moves away from the barre and progresses to the "center." The "center" consists of sequences of turns, balances, and jumps traveling across or around the studio. The Uzbek dancers started at the barre, doing the same exercises ballet dancers use at the beginning of a ballet barre. The Uzbek class moved to the center and the dancers performed rapid turns moving diagonally across the room. The footwork used for the turns was a variation of the ballet step called a *chaîné* turn.[4] The next sequence used arm and hand motifs characteristic of the Farghana dance style. The footwork and rhythms, however, were patterns used in Russian character dance (Anya Peterson Royce, personal communication). The classes I observed showed the impact of teachers trained in Moscow who brought their knowledge back to Uzbekistan.

Standardization and Nationalization

In addition to technical elaboration through incorporating ballet technique, the creation of a professional Uzbek dance form entailed designating a dance canon. Arjun Appadurai (1988) identified two processes in the formation of a national cuisine in India. The first is toward regionalization and standardization, as a simplified typology evolves for diverse local cuisines. The second process is the construction of a national cuisine, as elements from regional cuisines are combined in ways that cut across regional and ethnic boundaries.

In Uzbek national dances, similar processes of regionalization, standardization and nationalization occurred. During the 1930s and 1940s professional dancers developed three regional styles, one from each of the three historically important oases in Uzbekistan: Farghana, Bukhara, and Khorezm (see Chapter 3).

Returning to the three styles forming the official Uzbek dance canon, each style had its own distinctive repertoire of motifs, music, and costumes. One arts scholar, Roziya Karimova, eventually documented the three styles and notated many of the dances in a series of books. The books also constituted the basis of the five-year graded syllabus taught in the state choreographic school. The titles of her works show the taxonomy of Uzbek national dances:

Ferganskii Tanets (Farghana Dance) (1973)

Khorezmskii Tanets (Khorezmian Dance) (1975)

Bukharskii Tanets (Bukharan Dance) (1977)

Tantsyi Ansamblya <Bahor> (The "Spring" Dance Ensemble) (1979)

Uzbekskii Tantsye (Uzbek Dance) (1987; written with Isahar Akilov)

The books begin with sketches of seven characteristic positions of the arms and feet (*holat*). The identification of basic positions of the arms and feet was inspired by the Russian system for ballet training developed by Agrippina Vaganova. The positions of the arms and feet also bear striking resemblance to their counterparts in ballet technique.

The books notated some of the dances in each style, explaining the theme of the dance, the sequence of movement motifs, and directions of movement on the stage, and giving transcriptions of music for the dances. Photographs or sketches illustrated the costumes for each dance. The book on the *Bahor* Ensemble notated dances in the company's repertoire. The dances, music, and costumes associated with the three major regional styles were common knowledge: dancers and nondancers would often begin commentary on a dance by identifying the region the dance represented.

As for nationalization, dancers who recall the 1930s and 1940s complained that younger choreographers tended to mix movement motifs from the three regional styles in a single "national" dance. According to older dancers, the three regional styles comprising Uzbek dance were in danger of blurring into a single homogenous dance form. I heard that an arts scholar wrote a dissertation in the 1960s that pointed out that the styles had become so homogenized that only costumes and music distinguished dances purporting to be from different regions.

My own impressions changed as I studied Uzbek dance myself. At first the dances I saw on television and in concerts seemed virtually identical.

Pretty women with long black braids in sequined caftans skimmed the
stage with little running steps, arms curved softly over their heads, while
dainty hands fluttered like butterflies. The camera would zoom in as a
dancer paused, tilting her head and peeping archly at the audience out
of the corner of her eye.

I eventually learned four dances: two in the Bukharan style, and one
each in the styles of Farghana and Khorezm. Through dancing myself and
watching classes at the *maktab*, I began to see kinetic conventions distinguishing the regional styles. For example, in *Bukharcha* (Bukharan dance)
the dancer often did a back bend as she wriggled her shoulders in time
to the rapid pulse of the *doira* (drum).[5] Dancers told me *Bukharcha* originated in the court of the emirs of Bukhara, so it was flamboyant and
showy. The dancer's message was "Look at me!" One *Bukharcha* step I
learned mimed a dancer looking at herself repeatedly in a mirror.

Farghanacha (Farghana dance) usually involved curving, fluid, lyrical
arm movements and floor patterns. The gentle quality of *Farghanacha* expressed the Farghana Valley's fame as a fertile agricultural area. Most of
the land in Central Asia is a semiarid steppe zone; as a lush green region
by the Sur Daryo River, the Valley is highly prized. The names of Farghana
Valley motifs evoke the pastoral reputation of the region: *erik tolkin* (waves
of water), *nowda yiigilishi* (swaying trees), and *keghir buyin* (bird's neck).
The names of the steps were a recent invention: Karimova named many
of the movement motifs when she documented the different regional
styles and designated a systematic syllabus.

Other motifs in *Farghanacha* highlighted the beauty of the dancer. One
motif brought a hand to the dancer's lips as though she were eating a
piece of fruit (*labi guncha*, literally "sweet lips"). A second motif mimed
applying cosmetics to her eyebrows.[6] Farghana dances often had narrative
themes about romantic love. (See the discussion of *"Tanovar,"* Chapter
2.)

Whenever people discussed *Khorezmcha* (Khorezm dance), they began
to grin. One member of the intelligentsia said it was the "most Uzbek" of
the regional styles. Other people commented that in Khorezm, everyone
danced—men, women, children, and the elderly. Khorezmian dances impressed me as witty, spirited, and droll, unlike *Bukharcha* and *Farghanacha*
which were seldom humorous. In one dance I saw, boys crouched over
and swung their arms like elephant trunks. In another, old men in enormous puffy fur hats wobbled their heads from side to side as though they
were wooden dolls with necks made of springs.

The Khorezmian dance steps I learned from my teacher were iconic.
One hand motif imitated a candle flame, while another mimed picking
apples from a tree and dropping them in an apron. Khorezmian music
was the most syncopated and polyrhythmic of the three musical styles.

The steps generally skimmed over the music, forming yet another, almost independent, rhythmic layer.

Rhythm seemed to be the key to Khorezmian dance. As my teacher tried to teach me *Khorezmcha*, she became exasperated and made the dance simpler and simpler because I could not get the rhythm right. I remain perplexed and can say only that the music was in a ¾ meter, but the steps were not supposed to be on the downbeat nor on the upbeat. The closest I could get to satisfying my teacher was to fit the steps into a hemiola (a triplet against the ¾ meter) but stay slightly ahead of the music. A few months later I saw tiny children from Khorezm perform dazzling dance improvisations with rhythms so fast that their feet seemed suspended in midair.

The dance scholar's observation that all of the national dances looked alike had some basis but struck me as an overstatement. In the sphere of professional dance, decades of centralized dance training had produced a strong consensus about characteristics marking the regional styles. I observed students at the *maktab* learning examples of dances designated as *Bukhorcha, Farghanacha, and Khorezmcha* from teachers who had graduated from the *maktab* themselves. Within each dance style, choreographers used a specific and relatively limited lexicon of motifs. Films I saw from the 1940s used a wider variety of motifs, suggesting that innovation declined as the Uzbek dance canon evolved.

Some dances, especially those set to contemporary popular music (see Chapter 5) did draw freely on the lexicons of all three styles. Nevertheless, I also saw many dances old and new that were clear examples of a particular regional style. Over time each style seems to have become simplified into a stereotype of regional identity. Homogenization occurred more *within* a regional style, rather than across styles.

TWO PERSPECTIVES ON DANCE

The rehearsals for a concert performed on Independence Day demonstrated differences in the perspective of trained professional dancers and folkloric dancers. For the program, children from each of the thirteen provinces performed a dance representing their region. The pieces were prepared locally, then the children came to Tashkent for a month of rehearsals before the nationally televised concert performed on September 1. A team of prominent musicians and artistic directors from Tashkent oversaw the rehearsals and requested changes.

The piece I will discuss was choreographed by a teacher who was self-taught rather than a graduate of the choreographic school. She based the piece on ancient songs and dances from her region. About ten boys and girls about ages nine through twelve danced, sang, and chanted. The dancers formed two arcs, and one by one a boy or a girl would perform a brief solo to the music provided by the other children. I had observed a similar use of space at weddings, where the dancers would congregate into several roughly circular clusters and one or two dancers would briefly dance in the middle before yielding center stage to another dancer. The scene looked like a life-cycle celebration. Discussions with the Tashkent rehearsal team confirmed that the theme of the work was a *"töy"*—a social celebration such as a wedding or cradle party for a new baby.

During the course of the rehearsal period, the Tashkent team simplified the spatial structure of the dance, so that the children formed a single orderly arc around the rim of the stage. A group of five boys clustered stage right to form a focal point. Two boys performed energetic solos, one punching the air with his arms and slowly sinking to a kneeling position. The second boy followed in friendly rivalry, spinning in place like a top.

The Tashkent team also shaped the movement motifs. Before their input, each dancer moved in a slightly different way at a slightly different tempo. The dance had a casual, almost improvisational quality because each dancer followed a different impulse. For example, girls standing in the arcs around soloists moved in time to the music. Some shuffled their feet, others raised one arm over the head, then lowered it, and then raised the other arm. The choreographer from the Tashkent team got up on the stage one day and showed the girls specific movements from the Farghana professional dance vocabulary, and drilled them until they moved in unison to a marked ¾ meter. By the end of the rehearsal period, the dance had become a hybrid of the children's songs and games and the more geometric precision and uniformity of the professional dance presentation.

COMMODITIZATION

The standardization, regionalization, and nationalization of Uzbek dance can also be seen as a process of commoditization. A number of scholars have raised issues about the interpretation of material culture, or conversely about the consumption of symbols. In a capitalist context, scholars such as Davydd Greenwood (1977) have discussed how tourism affected community rituals. Greenwood explained how residents of the Basque community Fuenterrabia reenacted the "sacred history" of the town's resistance against the French siege in 1638. Greenwood argued that the *Alarde* was a ritual held for the townspeople to express the shared values of egalitarianism and "collective nobility." When the *Alarde* began to receive attention as a tourist event, the municipal government decreed that the *Alarde* be held twice in one day to accommodate spectators. The townspeople felt that turning the *Alarde* into a commercial event destroyed its meaning and became reluctant to participate.

Like the *Alarde*, Uzbek dances were initially rituals held for the participants, not the general public. For Uzbeks, the dances were usually part of life-cycle events, such as cradle parties. When the Soviet state put Uzbek dances on the stage, the Soviet state fundamentally changed the nature of the dances. Like raw materials undergoing manufacturing processes, the dances became more elaborate, incorporating Russian ballet and character dance techniques. Once the dances were turned into a finished "product" the Soviet State displayed them to foreigners as tokens of the Uzbek national character.

After the close of World War II, "national" dances became aesthetic "commodities" exported from Uzbekistan to Moscow and abroad for the benefit of the Soviet empire. From the dancers' perspective, a tour abroad was the acme of their career. Many dancers I interviewed began their career histories by reciting a list of countries where they had performed. Some toured with Uzbek dance companies, such as the *Bahor* Ensemble. Others toured with companies such as the Moiseyev State Academic Folk Dance Ensemble, which featured artists from all over the Soviet Union. Igor Moiseyev, a former Bolshoi choreographer, formed the ensemble in 1936 inspired by an All-Union Festival of Folk Dance in Moscow (Swift 1968: 244).

Moiseyev's comments about the political dimension of his company's touring illustrate how national dances became emblems of Soviet identity abroad:

I think that in our days artistic prestige is inseparable from political prestige. In any case, our art, which would appear to be quite remote from political passions, could not exercise such a strong aesthetic and emotional influence if it were not so politically well-defined and purposeful, if it were not Soviet art in the fullest sense of the term.

The audiences of our performances abroad judge us not only by our choreography and artistic skill. Above all they judge us as representatives of our country, our people, the art of the Soviet Union as a whole. And we like to tell of our people, so fond of life and straightforward, so proud and sincere; we enjoy telling at the top of our voices what kind of people our fellow countrymen are. We take pride in our political mission. (Moiseyev 1962: 156, quoted in Swift 1968: 247)

TELEVISION AND REFLEXIVITY

The Soviet government, then, fostered the development of an Uzbek national dance form and "exported" it to engender good will toward the USSR. Unlike the residents of Fuenterrabia, however, Uzbeks I observed in 1992 and 1994 did not abandon their enthusiasm for indigenous expressive arts when the state tried to appropriate them as resources. Instead, I saw creative responses that reappropriated new idioms introduced by the Uzbek government. The influence of television on social dances and wedding and life-cycle celebrations provided an example of resourcefulness.

The Uzbek government had its own television station. There were three stations in Uzbekistan: Uzbek, Turkish, and Russian. The Turkish and Russian broadcasts were available only in the evenings.[7] Programs about Uzbek culture dominated broadcasts on the Uzbek television station. The Uzbek television station had its own dance company, orchestra, and a staff dedicated to producing programs about Uzbek culture. To give an idea about the prominence of programs featuring the arts on the Uzbek station, the programs for a week chosen at random (December 12–18, 1994) included eight concerts, nine programs about particular Uzbek artists (performers and craftsmen), two plays, and several programs about Uzbek literature (*Gapiramiz wa Korsatamiz* 12.12–18.12, no. 50, 1994 *yil*).

Uzbeks I met who were not involved with the arts had mixed reactions toward the national dances. All were quite proud of their national artists. One *kolkhoz* worker in a rural area told me about the life of a well-known Uzbek professional dancer. She said she had seen a program about the dancer on television. When I visited Uzbek families, they would often turn on the national television station because they knew I was interested in dance. I thought everyone enjoyed the programs as much as I did until one polite acquaintance muttered, "Thank God," at the end of a lengthy dance and music program.

As I got to know people better I learned that foreign soap operas and movies were more popular fare than locally produced programs on the arts. Visits and household chores were suspended for the evening ritual of watching the Mexican soap opera *Simply Maria* (*Prosto Maria*). Some men rolled their eyes or scoffed at women's enthusiasm for Maria and Rosa, but whenever I raised the current soap opera in conversation, they all knew the latest plot developments. Other popular television programs included Turkish musical variety shows and Russian detective films.

Despite preferences for foreign television shows, Uzbek television had an impact on individual social dance practices and celebrations. I met a teenage girl in 1992 who danced for me in her living room while her mother plucked and strummed a *dutar*. The daughter enjoyed watching professional Uzbek dance programs on television and incorporated movements she liked into her own dancing. One parent praised her toddler when she began to rock from side to side trying to imitate little girls who were performing Uzbek dances on television.

Turning to life-cycle celebrations such as weddings and cradle parties, television inspired a reciprocal objectification of the events through videotaping. In 1992, one very wealthy family proudly showed me the videotape of their son's wedding on the VCR in their dining room. By 1994, nearly every wedding I went to had at least one and sometimes two videographers recording the proceedings, even if the family had no VCR.

One family came to my house to see a videotape I had made of their daughter's wedding. Although as hostess, I spent nearly the entire time in the kitchen cooking, the few comments I did hear identified people appearing on the television screen at the moment. By the time I left in December 1994, some families even managed to have videotapes of their celebrations broadcast on national television. At the state level, television broadcasts can be seen as a commoditization of professional Uzbek dance. At the household level, Uzbeks I met coopted television broadcasts about cultural events as idioms for recognizing family and community identities and values enacted in life-cycle celebrations.

CONCLUSION

This chapter examined how the institutionalization of Uzbek dance led to a centralized system of production, the creation of a standardized dance technique, and the construction of regional styles constituting "Uzbek" national dance. The professional national dancers performed in state-sponsored venues, for official occasions such as national holidays, or broadcasts on the national television station.

The process of nationalizing Uzbek dance traces Soviet efforts to legitimize a change from an indigenous model of collective identity defined in terms of agnatic kinship to a second, Soviet model of colonial development and exploitation of Uzbek national resources. Two expressive forms emerged: social dances performed by individuals in private settings, such as weddings, and the classical national dances.

The nationalization of Uzbek dance resembled a transformation Michael Herzfeld (1992: 99) noted in Crete, where carefully crafted bags marking a bride's new kinship ties to her husband's family became plainer "Greek" bags sold to tourists. To use Herzfeld's phrase, a shift occurred from the "genealogical to the generic" (1992: 99). The change in the design of the bags reflected a change from a patrilineal mode of determining kinship at a local level to a cognatic approach at the national level.

Nationalizing and standardizing Uzbek dances manipulated symbols of fundamental bases of Central Asian identity. Kinship, ethnicity, and geographical identity are strongly linked in Central Asian history. For example, people from Bukhara were often of Tajik (Persian) descent, while people from the Farghana Valley region were more likely to be of Uzbek and, hence, Turkic descent. Moreover, a person's geographic origin often indicated family ties. I visited one *kolkhoz* where a young woman told me that everyone in the village was a relative. Even in Tashkent, I met several families where brothers lived in houses on the same street. The homogenization of Uzbek local dance forms, then, also reshaped markers of ethnic and family identities. Kinship at the local level, defined by patrilineal relationships, merged into broader regional identities. "National" dancers embodied and enacted an Uzbek "family" comprised of the peoples of the three major Uzbek regions.

NOTES

1. See Michael Herzfeld (1992: 99).

2. Campbell described administrative hierarchies within the Soviet economy as a pyramid, rather than the core and periphery model I am using here. He identified sector (i.e., a kind of production) and function, in addition to territory, as factors in allocating authority (1991: 22–30).

3. The social organization of Bukharan dance probably differs from the structure of professional Uzbek dance in Tashkent because dance in Bukhara is often a family profession. I heard of several families of dancers in Bukhara, but additional research was not feasible in 1994 due to difficulties in obtaining local travel authorizations.

4. In a *chaîné* turn, the dancer spins while traveling in a straight line. The dancer remains poised on the balls of the feet (*relevé*), with the legs rotated outward and the feet about eight inches apart (first position). To reduce centrifugal force (and avoid getting pulled off balance) the arms are generally held in a tight circle in front of the dancer's body at the level of the breastbone.

In the Uzbek class, the dancers varied the *chaîné* turn as follows (instructions are for turns to the right):

1. Step *flat* on the right foot (rather than on the ball of the foot) in the direction of travel, turning the body about a quarter turn (ninety degrees) to the right.

2. Step *flat* on the left foot in the direction of travel, turning about another quarter turn (ninety degrees) to the right.

3. Place the ball of the right foot by the instep of the left foot and use it as a pivot for the last half of the turn (180 degrees) to the right. Put most of the body's weight on the right foot, but keep a bit of weight on the left foot and let it slide around the ball of the right foot.

Skillful Uzbek dancers can execute these turns very rapidly with a wide variety of stylized arm motifs. In learning these turns I found that the technique of using the right foot as a pivot (see 3 in instructions) gave greater stability and momentum than the ballet technique for a *chaîné* turn. The Uzbek approach, therefore, facilitated faster turns and more extensive elaboration of arm motifs than the balletic technique for a *chaîné* turn.

5. A *doira* resembles a large tambourine and is usually, but not always, played by men rather than women. The player evokes a variety of timbres from the flat head of the *doira*, by striking it closer to the edge or to the center. Small metal discs around the edge of the *doira* add a higher secondary timbre. See also note 2 in Chapter 3.

6. Dark, heavy eyebrows are an important feature of a woman's beauty. Eyebrows that meet in the middle to form a single horizontal line across the brow are con-

sidered very desirable. Many women in Uzbekistan use makeup to emphasize their eyebrows.

7. A commercial cable company had also begun offering access to a full spectrum of international stations, but the monthly cost exceeded my budget and that of most Uzbeks.

5

Independence (1991–1994)

During the Soviet period the roles of national dancers and dances changed. Once an informal practice at social events such as life-cycle celebrations, dance became a medium for creating a national and Soviet consciousness under the Soviet State. Dance became a cultural commodity that the state refined, produced, and presented to audiences. After World War II, Uzbek dance was displayed to other members of the Soviet and international community to celebrate Soviet unity.

Uzbekistan declared independence from the Soviet Union in 1991. This chapter presents the life histories of three young women to illustrate some of the new problems and opportunities of political independence. I then present a survey of dance events I observed in 1994 to explore new avenues Uzbeks were exploring and negotiating through the arts.

NASIBA AND LEILA

Dancers were among the first Uzbek participants in Soviet programs to recruit women as workers. Dance became a means of upward mobility and financial independence for women who danced during the Soviet period. The dancers I interviewed between the ages of about thirty-five to seventy often chose husbands who supported their careers, or left unsatisfactory marriages. Their careers gave them opportunities for travel, official and popular recognition of their talents, and, for some, considerable income.

The opportunities for young dancers in independent Uzbekistan were less rosy. The women I interviewed were carefully renegotiating their identities to cope with inflation and a more Islamic cultural climate. The life history of one young dancer I shall call Nasiba illustrates some of the choices young dancers faced in 1994.

I met Nasiba several times at rehearsals for various concerts. I inter-

viewed her informally while we sat in the shadowy wings of a theater while
we watched rehearsal. Nasiba's father was a businessman from the capital
city of Tashkent. She was the first artist in the family. She became interested in dance through television. Other dancers I interviewed became
interested, through dance training, in public school curriculum or seeing
Indian musical films. At age ten, she began studying at the children's
professional school in Tashkent. Although Nasiba was able to live at home,
the school also provided dormitory housing for children from outlying
provinces.

At seventeen, Nasiba graduated from the choreographic school and entered one of the major companies in Tashkent. She had been with the
company over ten years and looked forward to retiring with a pension.
Her career path traces the foundations established during the Soviet period: centralized professional training from childhood, followed by employment in a national dance company with the prospect of the financial
security of a pension. Nasiba married a fellow artist. They now have one
child, cared for by her mother while she works.

Nasiba would like to stop working to have more children, but she and
her family need her income. In Uzbekistan, the dancers received a salary
equivalent to about ten dollars (250 som) per month for their work with
the government-sponsored company. The dancers earned the same wages
regardless of the number of performances or hours worked. When I gathered this data on wages, I was spending about five dollars (135 som) per
week on groceries. Ten dollars per month was hardly adequate for basic
expenses. Like nearly everyone I met in Uzbekistan during 1994, the dancers were hard-pressed to cover their living expenses because their salaries
lagged far behind inflation.

To supplement their scanty incomes, some dancers took second jobs in
other fields, or extra work for special events. For example, one male dancer I met performed with a popular music singer for a concert in Tashkent, earning about ten times his monthly wages from the dance company
in a single weekend. His dance company used to forbid the dancers from
taking extra work. However, with the pressures of spiraling inflation as
Uzbekistan entered the world market, the moonlighting rule was relaxed
to help the dancers make ends meet.

Some dancers dreamed of traveling abroad to dance or teach. Even a
short visit would provide a chance to accumulate extra income. Many
dancers and teachers were abroad in 1994, lured by the prospect of travel
and earning generous wages in foreign currency.

For Nasiba and her husband, independence brought severe financial
pressures. It also brought the unprecedented hope of working indepen-
dently abroad. Nasiba's story also illuminates norms about gender in post-
Soviet Uzbekistan. Nasiba was fortunate to marry another artist, greatly

facilitating her ability to continue her career after marriage. Her success highlights the dilemma of Leila, another young dancer.

I met Leila while observing rehearsals for a concert. The director of her company made a point of introducing us when I began to watch the rehearsals. She always had a friendly smile and a hello for me so I asked her if she would be willing to be interviewed.

To thank her for the interview I invited her to lunch. Dining out was a rare event in Uzbekistan. People usually entertained at home (see Introduction) or brought food to work. Eating out was something foreigners or the very wealthy did. Leila was pleased and curious to try eating in a restaurant.

We went to a shop in the heart of Tashkent after a morning of rehearsals. The store offered imported goods such as chocolate, cosmetics, and embroidered nightgowns from China. One end of the shop sold *larmon* (long fat noodles in an oily broth of lamb, carrots, onions, and garlic). At the dingy counter we got glasses of hot tea, bread, and steaming bowls of *larmon*. We carried them to a nearby section with small tables and chairs. After we had eaten, I put my tape recorder on the table and we began the interview.

Leila was the daughter of a couple who worked in their own store selling a variety of state-manufactured goods such as clothing. She had one older sister, who was married and worked in a government department store, and three younger siblings. One was studying to become a medical assistant and the others were still in school.

Well since my childhood, since kindergarten, I was interested in that art [dance]. Then in elementary and secondary schools [*maktablar*]. In those children's clubs. When I learned my first dance it was for the republic province [*oblast*]. Next they gave many things in the dances. Then that reason was over. My parents had a talk with those girls. Our girls, they said, are those who will come to Tashkent to study the high arts. In this way for me the interest became lasting. After I came and after I studied I graduated. I am working now. Now I have been working happily.

Leila faced difficult decisions. At twenty-four, she was becoming old for marriage. Her mother was urging her to stop dancing and come home, where her family could help arrange a marriage for her. Her family was also concerned because dancing did not provide Leila with enough income to live. Leila wanted to continue performing and eventually become a *ballet mester* (choreographer/artistic director).

For example, after our graduation, for example here the example of my own . . . ensemble, if you put on a dance it is fine. Here I am able to put on a dance for the big stage. Secondly, us, we were taught for five years. We have become ballet masters. Like Kunduz Mukarrimova [former artistic director of the *Bahor* Ensemble]. . . . Now we have strength—after becoming a dancer not more than one has left. . . . For that reason after understanding a few of the dance patterns then I may work as a ballet master putting on dances. If I stay with the ensemble, I will put on dances. While I am dancing here I understand the choreography. I am a dancer as well. I also pursued advanced study of art [*madaniyat olii öqidim*]. I am also a ballet master.

Despite her training and ambitions, she was reluctantly considering leaving the stage to marry or go into more lucrative work.

Leila's difficulties may have arisen in part from questions about working women that seemed to grow stronger during 1994. When I first arrived in February 1994, young women told me they were able to work, thanks to benefits such as affordable and pleasant day care the government provided for children. By the time I left one young woman in graduate school said, "Our women are returning to the home." Some women said the day-care centers were not clean; others expressed concern about the growing delinquency rates among teenagers. Several friends planned to complete their graduate level work, then marry and raise children.

Comments like these suggested that Soviet programs to change the lives of women had only a limited effect on changing indigenous Muslim norms. Elizabeth Fernea ([1965] 1989: 56) found that Muslim women in an Iraqi village in the 1950s should be attractive, modest, fertile, and know how to cook well. Her husband was responsible for seeing that she behaved virtuously ([1965] 1989: 263). Similarly, "good" Uzbek women in the 1990s should behave modestly, marry, have children, and care for their families. The life history of a bride, Gulsara, shows that some young Uzbek women continue to take more traditional paths.

GULSARA

Gulsara had recently graduated from high school (*olii maktab*) and was about eighteen years old. I interviewed her a few days after her wedding. With shy pride she invited me into her "house"—a room in the family compound (*howli*) for the exclusive use of her and her new husband. The room was furnished with her dowry, including a low vanity with a huge mirror and towering stacks of folded quilts (*körpas*) made of *atlas* (ikat-patterned fabric). She invited me to sit on a *körpa* made of metallic gold fabric spread out on the floor. As I sat down, a strong smell of sweat and musk rose like a cloud. Perhaps this was how a bride provided tacit proof of the happy consummation of her marriage.

Gulsara: I was born in the Republic of Kyrgyzstan. The family of my mother was from Kyrgyzstan. I was born there then we came to W*** province. After being born, growing up, living, I study at the institute. . . . The first year.

MD: Do you have any brothers or sisters?

Gulsara: Uhhuh. There are four children. One boy and three girls. I have an older sister. She is married. Then the second child is a son, then my younger sister.

MD: Is she in school now?

Gulsara: She is in school. My younger brother graduated from the *maktab*. He is working.

MD: What does he do?

Gulsara: Businessman [*kommersant*] . . .

MD: You said that you study at the institute. What classes do you take?

Gulsara: Uzbek language, Russian language, literature. When we finish the fifth course we will enter teaching.

Her parents were relatives. Gulsara had grown up near the groom and was related to him through her father's side of the family.

MD: How did your family come from Kazakhstan (Gulsara corrects me—Kyrgyzstan) to W*** province?

Gulsara: My father was working there. My father was Uzbek. My mother was in Kyrgyzstan. They were married in Kyrgyzstan then we came to Uzbekistan.

MD: How did your mother marry [your father]?

Gulsara: They were relatives. . . .

MD: Are you and your husband relatives too?

Gulsara: Uh-huh. Relatives.

MD: What is the connection?

Gulsara: On my father's side. I married my father's side. . . . An uncle (unintelligible).

MD: You live nearby?

Gulsara: Our house is nearby. Since it is new, they will stay here.

The groom was the son of a retired politician. The groom's older sister had suggested Gulsara as a potential bride for her brother and was quite proud that she had "found" the bride.

The verb "to marry" in Uzbek highlights important aspects of gender in Uzbek society. For grooms, the verb *"uylanmok"* means "to marry." It is related to the noun *"uyi,"* meaning "house." As the phrase suggests, the groom and his family are responsible for providing housing for the newlyweds. Traditionally, the youngest son and his bride care for his aging parents and eventually inherit the family compound. Older sons and their brides may live with the family until they can afford their own homes, others may receive separate quarters from their parents upon marriage.

For brides, however, the verb for marriage is *"turmushka chikmok"*—"to go out into life." An unmarried female of any age is considered *"qiz"*—a girl, rather than *"hotin"*—a married adult woman. The bride's family must provide her with an extensive wardrobe and all the furnishings for the home her husband will provide. A single woman's marginal status is underscored by the Uzbek adage: "A daughter is a guest in her parent's home." In other words, parents raise a daughter only to give her away after considerable expense.

The wedding consisted of a gathering at the bride's home for her male relatives in the morning, followed by an evening celebration at the bride's home. The next day, the groom would come to the bride's house and take her to his home for yet another celebration for his relatives and friends of his family. The portion of the ceremony I will focus on is called the *yuz ochish* (opening of the bride's face). Held the morning after the bride has been brought to the groom's home, the ceremony is attended only by the groom's female relatives. I was thus very fortunate to see this event.

The ceremony began in the bride's "house"—the room in the groom's family compound where the newlyweds would live. New clothing and tapestries from the bride's dowry lined the walls. One side of the room displayed Western-style ensembles, while the other held traditional dresses made of *atlas*. The guests sat on the floor around large tablecloths (*dasturhon*) covered with trays of pastries and cookies baked and contributed by the guests. Seating followed status in the family, based principally on age. The elderly women in the groom's family held places of honor at the head of the table. The other women sat in descending order of age, with the oldest near the head of the table and the youngest toward the foot of the table.

The *yuz ochish* ceremony followed the familiar three-stage process of rites of passage: separation, liminality, and reaggregation (Turner 1967). While the women in the groom's family feasted, the bride remained secluded with a close friend or two behind a tent made of an embroidered hanging. Her mother sat next to the tent so her daughter could whisper to her.

After clearing the feast, the women went out into the sunny courtyard of the groom's house. While the musicians played and sang folk songs, the women stood or sat in a circle. One by one they entered the center of the circle and danced exuberant solos. The excitement and laughter built as each dancer strove to top the others. Particularly graceful or spirited steps won accolades of small bills or lengths of fabric. The dancers usually gave the money and fabric to the musicians.

I stood to one side taking photographs and each dancer turned to make sure I would take her picture. I was finally dragged out from behind my camera and urged into the center of the circle. The groom's sister entered the circle to show me some steps and I began to mirror her movements. The women began to clap and drape fabric around our necks, urging us to bolder and more complex movements until we were both whirling around the courtyard. The dance ended as the laughing circle of women patted us on the arms, saying, "Well done, well done." I had learned to move carefully and with restraint in Uzbekistan, but on this one afternoon, I tasted a heady blend of freedom and *communitas* spiced with friendly competition.

Dancing, however, was a complex and compartmentalized practice. The spontaneity of the dancing at the *yuz ochish* contrasted with the dancing at the wedding feast the night before. I had seen many of the same women at the wedding feast attended by about 300 of the male and female relatives and friends of the groom's family. Women had generally avoided being the center of attention by chatting at tables on the side of the courtyard or dancing in small clusters of three or four. It was the men who had commanded the dance floor and the eyes of the guests with distinctive solos. It seems that in mixed company, women behaved congenially but modestly. In the setting of the *yuz ochish*, however, surrounded by a small group of close female relatives and friends, the women vied for attention with sparkling displays of skill and creativity.

The two-edged nature of dance[1] became even more apparent when one of the hostesses told me that she had been a close friend of Mukarram Turghunbayeva, one of the very first professional dancers in Uzbekistan (see Chapter 2). The dance she did at the *yuz ochish* feast was inspired by what she had learned about dance from Turghunbayeva. Her daughter wanted to become a dancer in Turghunbayeva's company. My hostess's husband, a member of the intelligentsia, told his daughter not to become a dancer because it was a frivolous (*yengil*) profession. The daughter eventually chose a career in academia instead. Nevertheless, her dancing skill won warm applause and many gifts of cloth and money from the women at the *yuz ochish*. The older women went into the courtyard and danced while the younger women cleared the remains of the feast. When the dishes had been cleared away, the guests returned and began to sing for the bride. Head bowed under a white lacy veil, the bride emerged from the tent. A woman unveiled the bride.

The bride crossed the room to sit across from an older male relative of the groom.[2] She held out her hands while he filled them with rice from a heap on the floor. Some people said her hands were filled with rice so she would always have food to feed her family; others said it was because she would be doing the cooking. The ceremony ended as the bride's new relatives embraced her one by one. They also picked her up as they hugged her. I was told to embrace her too, but that I did not have to pick her up. When I hoisted her anyway, everyone laughed.

Two days after the wedding, the young bride had assumed her new domestic responsibilities. Head wrapped in a pretty kerchief, she was cheerfully sorting the family's laundry and filling a tub with water as I left for the train station.

Bride (in white scarf) emerging from embroidered "tent" at the end of *yuz ochish*
celebration.

Gulsara's path of a youthful marriage to a relative in her community
resembles life histories I gathered from very elderly women about times
before the Soviet reforms. The dance practices at the wedding and *yuz
ochish* also reveal substantial information about gender in Uzbek society.
Dancing skillfully was a source of social capital and camaraderie for men
as they performed on the dance floor in front of hundreds of male and
female guests. For men, attracting the gaze of the audience added to their
prestige. In private settings such as the wedding and *yuz ochish*, women
danced for personal prestige and pleasure. For women, dancing was a
source of social capital when they would be seen only by other women.
Dancing in front of men, at social events or on the stage, detracted from
a woman's social standing because a virtuous woman did not want to draw
the gaze of men. In groups involving women only, for married women,
dance was a medium for expressing personal style and creativity. Adolescent girls nearing the marriageable age of sixteen, however, danced with
restraint and shyness in order to please older women who might be searching for brides for sons or brothers.

Many women I met who came of age after several decades of Soviet rule
and are now in their forties and fifties were committed to ambitious careers and had relatively small families of one to three children. Their labor
in the workplace earned them prestige and financial independence.
Younger women, however, were renegotiating their identities in a rapidly

Young mother baking bread (one of many chores) in outside oven (*tandoor*).

changing economic and moral climate. Gulsara, the young bride, followed the traditional Central Asian path for women—an arranged marriage to a relative from her neighborhood. Dancers like Nasiba were attempting to juggle a career and marriage. For those who have yet to marry like Leila, the uncertainties brought by independence made their choices even more difficult.

The lives of Nasiba, Leila, and Gulsara show the increased repertoire of choices young women have, ranging from the traditional Central Asian path of marriage to a relative through combining marriage and a career or travel abroad. Nasiba and her husband sought to make the most of the new economic opportunities independence opens by taking work in privately sponsored concerts or perhaps even teaching and performing abroad. The choices available to young women were an amalgam of Central Asian traditions, Soviet programs to bring women into public life and new options created by global exchanges afforded by Uzbekistan's political independence.

NATIONAL DANCES

Looking at the social field of dance reveals a similar proliferation in the repertoire of choices following Uzbekistan's political independence. The dances I saw drew on the same trio of resources: indigenous Central Asian history, Soviet reforms, and the contemporary global marketplace of images and ideas. During my field research in 1992 and 1994, I observed professional dancers performing at international conferences, national holidays, school children's visits, and regularly scheduled concerts in state theaters. Professional dancers would occasionally appear at commercial concerts by musicians or in honor of organizations like the Red Crescent. Studying several examples of national dance performances suggests emerging themes in the ways some Uzbek artists interpreted and responded to independence.

RENEGOTIATING NATIONAL IDENTITY

The most spectacular example of national dance I saw was at the 1994 Independence Day Concert. The concert was a massive, nationally televised production sponsored by the government. The concert resulted from a coordinated effort cutting across national, regional, and local lines. The Ministry of Culture planned the program months in advance, then commissioned dancers, actors, and musicians to create works in accordance with the plan. The performers included hundreds of children from each province of Uzbekistan and scores of well-known professional dancers and musicians. The performers rehearsed five to six days a week during the month of August. Local and national leaders reviewed the dress rehearsal and specified changes. The content of the program was directed and approved by state officials.

Independence Day concerts had been given twice before, once in 1992 and a second time in 1993. I had the good fortune to observe and videotape rehearsals during most of the month of August 1994 and to observe this new Uzbek tradition in the making. The concert was a splendid collection of representations of "Uzbek" national identity in the newly independent republic.

The two-hour program consisted of three parts. First, a capsule history of the nation from medieval times to the present portrayed through drama, dance, and music. The historical section referred to the Central Asian scholar-statesment Ulughbeg (circa 1394–1449), and to the opening of the Farghana Canal, a major landmark of Soviet modernization. The second portion of the program featured musical presentations by children from each of the nation's provinces, and the third segment featured some of the country's most famous professional popular singers and musicians. The three major portions of the program drew on Uzbekistan's ancient Central Asian past, Soviet reforms, and popular culture as resources to represent Uzbekistan to a national television audience and a live audience of 10,000 local and foreign dignitaries.

The 1994 Independence Day celebration provided a forum for recognizing far more than three regional identities. Dances and songs acknowledged minority ethnic groups such as Korean, Russian, and Tajik, as well as all thirteen provinces. Emigration of skilled minority workers from Uz-

Young women in Uzbek national dress celebrate Central Asian scholar-statesman Ulughbeg's 600th birthday in 1994.

bekistan had been a major concern during 1994. The concert carefully acknowledged many minority groups. One of the dramatic highlights of the concert was a tribute to a blacksmith and his wife who had adopted children of every Soviet nationality during World War II. The reminder was clear: all peoples were members of the Uzbek national family.

To Uzbeks I met, however, dances and concerts had two simpler meanings. Dances were "pretty" and enjoyable events. Invitations to concerts on official holidays were markers of status: noted politicians, dignitaries, members of the intelligentsia, and World War II veterans received tickets. The guest list therefore designated and affirmed a social hierarchy.

In the days before the concert, tickets were in great demand. Three people involved with presenting the program promised me tickets to the actual concert, but competition for tickets was so intense that I never received any. To my great disappointment, I was unable to see the actual performance. Even without tickets I wanted to go to *Mustaqillik Maydoni* (Independence Square), the central square where the concert would be held, but Uzbek friends told me that it would be dangerous to be out on the festival night and advised me not to go. I did tape the live television broadcast.

I asked several people whether the Independence Day concert differed from celebrations on holidays during the Soviet period. I found people curiously reluctant to discuss the old Soviet holidays. One dancer told me

Musicians in *döppilar* (Uzbek caps) perform at a feast in honor of Ulughbeg's birthday in 1994.

that there used to be events involving many people on the holidays but concerts featuring children were new. Another young woman in her twenties said that the opening number of the Independence Day concert reminded her of the kinds of displays that occurred during the Soviet period. The presentation in the 1994 concert featured row upon row of people carrying flags in the colors of the national flag of Uzbekistan: white, orange, green, yellow, and blue. The flag bearers marched, wheeled, and dipped their flags in time to a swelling crescendo of sound from a recording of a mixed chorus.

One official influential in cultural affairs characterized the celebrations of Soviet holidays as *demonstrasiya* (demonstrations). In fluent, elegant Uzbek, he enthusiastically described the new calendar of holidays the independent Uzbek government had adopted. The calendar included new holidays such as Independence Day (September 1) and holidays like *Navruz*, an ancient celebration of spring, which had been discouraged during the Soviet period. While I was in Uzbekistan, the Soviet holiday in honor of women and girls (March 8) was still observed. The new calendar was thus a hybrid of old and new celebrations.

CONTESTED REPRESENTATIONS

Despite lavish rituals like the Independence Day concert, dance was a site of contests about how national identity should be represented. At least two movements were evident in the social field of dance. One was a trend towards "purifying" Uzbek dance by returning to traditional themes. A second encouraged innovation. Turning to "purification," choreographers worked within a single regional canon rather than mixing the movement vocabularies of all three regional styles.

For example, I saw several renditions of dances called *"munojot."* The *munojot* is both a poetic form and a musical genre. Poets wrote *munojot* as prayers to God. The version familiar to dancers in Uzbekistan was set to poetry by the fifteenth-century poet Alisher Navoi. One *munojot* I saw in 1994 was staged for a concert performed to commemorate the day that Uzbekistan adopted its own constitution as an independent republic. The choreographer was Kunduz Mukarrimova, the former director of the famous dance ensemble founded by Mukarram Turghunbayeva.

I heard that Mukarrimova was particularly excited about this version because it was a "big" *munojot* using thirty-eight dancers. A dancer involved in the production told me that Mukarrimova's version contained several original touches. For example, pairs of dancers raised their arms to form arches to suggest a *madrasa* (a place of study for Muslim scholars). *Madrasas* usually have many arched doorways, leading into small private cells for the scholars. In rehearsal, the dancers forming the archways were men, perhaps even Navoi, and the women emerging through the portals might have been his beautiful dream. At the last minute, however, perhaps due to problems in finding costumes for the men, the male dancers were replaced with women.

The *munojot* performed on Constitution Day (December 6) was thus a tribute to a great Central Asian literary figure and a sophisticated musical tradition. The allusion to *madrasas* further acknowledged the rich intellectual heritage of the Uzbek people, as well as their piety. It may be no coincidence that the dance was created and performed shortly after the government launched a new slogan "Culture and Piety" (*madaniyat wa ma'rifat*).

The dance itself was slow and stately. A single female vocalist with a low, resonant voice carved the downward contours of the melody, etching syllables with elaborate turns and ornamentation. The time line, marked by a lone *doira* (drum), sounded like a dirge to me:

X		*	*	X		*	*	X

The dancers, echoing the vocal motifs, combined full sweeping arm movements with delicate flourishes of the wrists and hands. The gestures came from the lyrical vocabulary of the Farghana style. The costumes reminded me of miniature paintings I had seen in a museum display about the fifteenth-century Central Asian scholar-statesman Ulughbeg. The vocalist and the female dancers wore floor-length, peacock-blue caftans with gold trim around the neckline and down the center of the torso. With each step, the dresses shimmered because they were made from material covered with sequins. Peaked jeweled tiaras framed the performers' faces.

With the Constitution Day *munojot*, the role of dance in Central Asian statecraft came full circle, from undermining the Muslim faith and values to officially acknowledging them. Dance was again an instrument of social reform in Uzbekistan, but this time to rebuild rather than to destroy a people. The irony is compounded by the fact that using *munojot* in a public dance performance, by women, would in all likelihood have been anathema to the pious poets who wrote *munojots* as prayers.

One official active in the arts criticized the professional national dancers and praised amateur folkloric performers. According to him, the amateur dancers and singers were untrained and their work was "natural" and in accordance with Islam because it was "God-given." He scorned the professional dancers, saying the training had made male dancers (and by implication, Uzbek men) effeminate.

GLOBAL CULTURE

At the other end of the spectrum, dances set to contemporary *estradni* (popular) music showed a second trend toward embracing innovation. *Estradni* music began in the 1970s when a group of musicians combined Uzbek folk melodies with Western electronic instruments and arrangements inspired by the Beatles. *Yalla* (Let's Go), the first and most famous *estradni* group consisted of male musicians. I saw them perform many times. The leader of the group had wavy hair to his shoulders and a mustache. The group wore Armani-style double-breasted suits, or floor-length sequined robes inspired by miniature paintings of Central Asian royalty. Most of the concerts I attended devoted about half of the program to *estradni* music.

Dancers often joined the musicians performing movements from the classical Uzbek dance lexicon to the contemporary music. I observed choreographers setting works to *estradni* music. They chose motifs corresponding to the meaning of the words. For example, one choreographer used the gesture of folding hands over her heart, then reaching out and shaking her head to illustrate the words "I will give [you] to no one" (*Meni seni hechkimga bermayman*).

The regional origin of the melody did not appear to be a factor in choosing the movement lexicon. Uzbeks of all ages enjoyed *estradni*. The syncretism of popular music led to rapid incorporation of new musical styles and sounds. MTV aired daily on television. In one of the last concerts I attended before I left in December 1994, *Yalla* sang verses by the fifteenth-century poet Navoi to a rap song.

CONCLUSION

With independence, Uzbeks have an increased range of choices that incorporate practices from indigenous Central Asian culture, Soviet "modernization," and new opportunities for work and travel abroad. Similarly, national dances retained some of the meanings acquired during the Soviet years, and took on still more. In the context of state rituals, such as Independence Day celebrations, dance was part of a display of Central Asian history. Dance was an index of Uzbekistan's rich cultural heritage.

I asked an official of the Ministry of Culture why the Uzbek government commemorated holidays with events like the Independence Day concert. He explained that events featuring the arts symbolized Uzbekistan's freedom from Soviet rule. During the Soviet period, Uzbek culture was suppressed. The flourishing of the arts signified the flourishing of the independent Uzbek people.

NOTES

1. In Greece, Jane Cowan (1990: 188–205) found dance was an ambiguous activity for women. Women wanted to dance well and show spirit. A woman who displayed too much flamboyance, however, drew censure for loose behavior.

2. Guests said he was the groom's *aka*. Literally *"aka"* means "elder brother," but I heard the term applied to other senior male relatives such as uncles or cousins.

Conclusion: "It Is We Who Own Uzbekistan Now"

Uzbek national dancers elaborated household and local dance motifs and codified them into a system of styles representative of Farghana, Bukhara, and Khorezm, the three major historical regions within the Uzbek borders. "Uzbek" came to mean an amalgamation of these three regions. As an institution, dance evolved from a controversial undertaking by some of the most marginal and powerless women to an established profession.

In this final chapter, I argue that it was the very marginality of dance that enabled dancers to make it a site of cultural production of "Uzbek" rather than "Soviet" symbols. I also conclude that the liminal status of "girls" in the Uzbek kinship system explains the efficacy of dancers as national symbols.

DISPLACEMENT AND LIMINALITY

It was a year and half after I returned from the field when I realized I had dismissed something crucial. Before the Soviet period, kinship and geography were the fundamental principles of social order. The region that became Uzbekistan was predominantly composed of sedentary agricultural populations. Geographical residence and kinship were so closely linked that to know someone's place of origin generally revealed their place in society as well.

Joelle Bahloul (1992) discovered a foundation of Jewish oral narrative forms in the poetic structure of the "collective autobiography" she gathered from her relatives. The stories dancers shared were not stories of continuous residence in a single location. Rather, they were narratives of displacement. The narrative form underlying the life histories was an itinerary. One dancer advised me whom to interview. "Don't bother with the others, they'll just tell you which countries they have been to." I found many dancers did exactly that—tell me where they were born, what their parents did, how many brothers and sisters they had. Then they would talk about coming to Tashkent to study dance, joining a company, and touring. The rest of the discussion would revolve around a list of stops on their tours.

Dancers in each professional generation experienced radical discontinuities. Many dancers in the 1930s were orphans, taken from local orphanages to Samarkand for dance training. For them, the tenuous ties with their natal communities were broken first by the loss of their parents, then severed when they began training as dancers. Mukarram Turghunbayeva left home to join Kari Yakubov's company. Tamara Khonim married Usta Kalimov and began performing with him and his musicians. Kari Yakubov recruited Karimova, an orphan, from her *teknikum* (technical school) at age fourteen and had her taken to Samarkand for training. For these women, their careers were essentially stories of journeys through the new institutions established during the early Soviet years: membership in dance companies, training in schools, and touring with their companies.

In the 1940s World War II interrupted dance training for Anna. Dilorum, along with a cohort of gifted children, went to Moscow for training. Her career severed her ties with Uzbekistan and took her to the hub of the Soviet empire in Moscow, then throughout the Soviet Union and then overseas as a member of a pan-Soviet performing group.

Moreover, Anna and Dilorum both emphasized the importance of training in the formation of a dancer. My observations of classes show that at least in 1994, dance classes were a symbolic journey through the major regions of the Uzbek-speaking peoples. Viewing dance classes in the children's choreographic school as a ritual, I argue that the classes were rituals of acculturation. The taxonomy of dance styles representing historically significant regions in Uzbekistan made each class a symbolic journey through the territory of the Uzbek republic.

Dancers joining the professional ranks in the 1950s and 1960s had opportunities for advanced training as directors and choreographers in Moscow, and some joined pan-Soviet companies. In the 1970s, until the fall of the Soviet Union, flagship Uzbek national dance companies toured internationally. In Chapter 4 I argued that the Soviet Union refined and "exported" Uzbek national dance as a "commodity" for display throughout the Soviet Union and abroad.

What does it mean that these dancers unfolded their stories as itineraries? Benedict Anderson (1983: 53–65) discussed the impact of repeated relocations on Creoles who worked for the Spanish colonial government in the Spanish Americas. Individuals who became civil servants left their local villages and spent their careers and lives moving through a series of posts in different towns and regions of the colonial territories. Their experiences outside of their villages gave them perspectives beyond those of their former relatives and neighbors. Nevertheless, because they were born in the Americas rather than Spain, they were never fully accepted by the Spanish colonial rulers. As a result of their "looping" career paths between the colonial capital and outlying posts, these individuals acquired a liminal status. They were neither Spanish nor permanent residents of a local community. They formed ties to each other and eventually became nationalists because they had a perspective that transcended local ties and the education and skills to build a nation.

Although the Uzbek dancers did not become revolutionaries like the Creole functionaries, they did come to occupy marginal social and geographic spaces. Their training and careers took them in spatial trajectories from regional cities and provinces to the central capital city of Tashkent, touring other Soviet republics, additional training in Moscow, and for the most fortunate, abroad. The first dance company was formed when the Soviets tried to rupture the fundamental Central Asian unities of family, place, and identity. With each generation, the alienation from family and natal community became more pronounced.

Karimova's generation severed ties to kin groups and local communities. Karimova told her story as a series of changes in place—from her birthplace to an orphanage, a foster home, dance school, and finally a series of theaters and schools where she worked. She remembered the years of events, or her age, only when prompted. Space and movement organized her recollections. Tamara Khonim's links to Uzbekistan were tenuous because she was of Armenian descent. Mukarram Turghunbayeva gave the day she left home to become a dancer as her birthday on official papers. The early dancers traveled throughout Uzbekistan and parts of the Soviet Union. They began to think of themselves as Uzbeks and as dancers in the newly formed SSR of Uzbekistan. In contrast, Firuza, the mountain bride, considered the years her family and in-laws were near as the happiest years of her life.

Dilorum's cohort went to Moscow as children. Dilorum spent most of her professional life as an artistic representative of Uzbekistan and a member of a Soviet troupe. She was thus an Uzbek and a Soviet citizen.

Dancers in the next generation toured the world as part of Uzbek dance companies and pan-Soviet companies. As each cohort's trajectories expanded to include a wider geographic scope, the bases of collective identities expanded as well. From members of kin groups and local communities, the dancers became representatives of Uzbekistan and finally the Soviet Union. The underlying "scenario," to use James Peacock and Dorothy Holland's (1993) term, of a journey thus provides a way to map the transformations in consciousness among the dancers and to trace the evolution of a national "Uzbek" identity.

MARGINALITY AND CONTROL OF SYMBOLS

Turning to the relationship of dancers to Uzbek society, their geographic and social marginality positioned them to become significant producers of Uzbek culture. For purposes of this discussion, Jean Comaroff's (1985) study of the Zionist sects in South Africa is a helpful point of departure. She showed how Zionists in South Africa used marginality as a physical and metaphorical device to define their relationship to the larger colonial community.

According to Comaroff, the Zionists combined elements of the indigenous Tshidi pantheon and rituals with Christian ideas and services to create their own distinctive religious sect. Marginality thus became a way of distinguishing themselves from both other Tshidi and the European colonists and missionaries. Practices such as siting their churches on the outskirts of communities, distinctive dress, and endorsement of (if not compliance with) endogamy within the church membership all enabled the members to carve out a region of partial influence and autonomy under a colonial regime.

Similarly, in Soviet Uzbekistan, dance became a social domain of at least partial autonomy for dancers, musicians, and choreographers. Although the performing groups were state-sponsored, and the artists employed and trained by the state, the life histories of the dancers and the dances themselves show that the national dance companies became a site where the Uzbek cultural heritage was honored and celebrated. Unpacking the ambiguous dynamics of Uzbek national dances entails looking at a crucial question Comaroff raised: the control of symbols. Comaroff said:

In fact, black religious innovation in southern Africa has likewise sought to wrest the Christian "message from the messenger" [citation omitted]; and its history has been peppered with battles over the control of master symbols, such as the "right" to baptize or dispense communion. (1985: 196–197)

Within the broader context of Soviet rule, Uzbek language and history were harshly suppressed during the Soviet period. One graduate student told me that during the Soviet period, *maktab* (school) students covered the history of Uzbekistan only one day a year. In 1994, scholars were just beginning the project of writing a multivolume history of Uzbekistan for use in schools. Russian, as the lingua franca of the Soviet Union, became the language of the educated elite.

The best schools were Russian language schools, and Russian was the language of scholarship and government. I attended a dissertation defense in 1994 that was the first defense conducted primarily in Uzbek. Until then, candidates wrote their theses and defended in Russian. One professor I spoke to in 1992 said Uzbek became the language of the home.

Uzbeks who could still speak the language after seventy years of Russian rule spoke "kitchen Uzbek."

Where, then, could Uzbek culture, literature, and language continue to thrive? Anya Peterson Royce (1982: 168–183) argued that "style"—clothing, music, dance, literature—can be a "strategy of ethnicity." Uzbek national dance companies were one social domain in which music, songs, costumes, and regional themes appeared freely. Uzbek national dancers became repositories of Central Asian poetry, dance, and music.

This is not to say that the forms remained unchanged. Uzbek national dance, as discussed in Chapter 4, was a hybrid form combining Russian ballet technique with indigenous movement motifs. Uzbek dancers colonized Russian ballet technique in service of creating a "national" dance form. They also maintained a significant degree of control over the creation, manipulation, and presentation of the symbolic content of the dances.

AGENCY

From the perspective of the dancers, the artists I interviewed were not fully aware, nor interested in, the policy implications of their work. Alternatively, if they did consider their work a form of protest or propaganda, they did not share these views with me. Karimova (see Chapter 2) did say that the dancers were supposed to show people "how to behave" and that dances in the 1940s, like the dance dramatizing the murder of Noor Khon, addressed the problems of liberating women. Nevertheless, she said, "We just danced. We lived for dance, we lived for art."

Dilorum (see Chapter 3) seemed aware that the dancers were an example to the extent that they had to be bigger than life and command the stage. Dancers in later cohorts chose dance because they loved to dance. The example of other national dancers or even Indian movie musicals attracted them to the profession.

Many dancers I met were fluent Russian speakers. Some were actually more fluent in Russian than Uzbek and spoke Uzbek to me and Russian to each other. Nevertheless, their comments about their work emphasized the importance of appreciating Uzbek life, people, and culture.

Uzbek national dances are intertwined with Uzbek poetry and music. Karimova said, "Dance is like poetry: it is just like a flower" (see Chapter 2). Many of the dances I saw were performed to songs with lyrics drawn from classical poetry. For example, the *munojot* performed on Constitution Day (see Chapter 5) was set to poetry by Alisher Navoi.

The interdependence of the Uzbek language, dance, music, and nationalist sentiment was dramatically illustrated in an audition I observed in 1994. I had the rare opportunity to observe a great Uzbek musician looking for a new dancer to perform with him. He asked the dancers to improvise movements expressing the lyrics of his songs. The lyrics, of course, were in Uzbek. (He asked me not to publish the lyrics, because the songs were new, so I cannot give a specific example of the lyrics.) The single dancer who pleased him used iconic gestures to dramatize his song. She folded her hands over her heart, then reached into the distance, turning shyly away to express love. He did, however, lecture the dancers at length on the necessity of knowing the Uzbek language in order to dance well. He said that if they knew Uzbek, dance would be easy. It would come from the heart.

There is a certain irony in the juxtaposition of dance and poetry. Public dance performances by women were unthinkable during the pre-Soviet period; such dance would have been profane. Poetry, on the other hand, has a proud heritage as a marker of the high cultural achievements of Central Asian empires. It also has connotations of the sacred from Sufi poets such as Jalāluddīn Rūmī (1207–1273). Dance performances set to poetry are thus a peculiar juxtaposition of the sacred and the profane.

One could argue that recontextualizing these "sacred" markers of Central Asian pride—history, literature, culture, and piety—into the "profane" space of the stage, tainted and degraded them. However, I contend that whatever the intention of the Soviet policy makers, the theater became one of the few places where this heritage could be remembered and appreciated in relative freedom. Just as the marginality of the Tshidi Zionists afforded them a measure of autonomy from the European colonists and missionaries, so the marginality of the stage enabled the national dance schools and companies to become sites for preserving Uzbekistan's cultural heritage.

GESTURE, GENDER, AND NATION BUILDING

Returning to the question I posed in the introduction of this book, why did dancers and dances become symbols of Uzbek national identity? As I discuss in Chapter 1, of the many roles women play, motherhood is perhaps the most important. Lineage is determined patrilaterally, but mothers are key figures in day-to-day life. Women give birth to their own empires. Due to early mortality of men, women become key decision makers in the lives of their children and grandchildren. Emotionally, relationships among fathers, children, and siblings are warm, but mentioning the bond between mother and child, even in the abstract, evokes a powerful emotional response, and often brings tears to the eyes.

Mothers are the heart of the Uzbek kinship system and domestic life. While a complete discussion of motherhood in Uzbek political culture is beyond the scope of this study, motherhood does play a significant role in national rhetoric. Songs and speeches pay homage to *watan* (the motherland). Motherhood received recognition as a service to the nation through the institution of "Hero Mothers." A woman becomes a Hero Mother when she bears ten children. On Women and Girls Day (March 8) and on Independence Day (September 1) I saw a Hero Mother who had seventeen children honored at a concert. A second Hero Mother appeared in a scene in the Independence Day concert remembering a couple who adopted children from all of the Soviet peoples during World War II.

In other societies, the powerful emotional affect of kinship made it a central symbol in the semiotics of nation building (see, e.g., Anderson, 1983: 143–144; Delaney 1995: 177–193). For example, Carol Delaney said that Mustafa Kemal, the founder of the twentieth-century Turkish republic, represented the nation as the marriage of the *Anavatan* (Motherland) and the *Devlet Baba* (Father State) in order to legitimize the concept of the nation-state as "a circumscribed body of land isomorphic with the body politic" (1995: 179, 187). Indeed, Kemal claimed the name *Ataturk* (father of the Turks) for his exclusive use. While further study of rhetoric during the Soviet period would be necessary, my preliminary data about motherhood suggests that the gendering of national discourse was quite different in Uzbekistan.

The meanings of the two terms *watan* and *davlat* bring out two aspects of nationhood. When people mentioned *watan* (the homeland or the motherland), their faces would soften into an affectionate, almost wistful smile, similar to the expression many people assumed when speaking of their own mothers. *Davlat* means the state or government. In contrast to *watan*, it seemed curiously devoid of emotional affect. Voices became carefully neutral, and faces bland. At most people would shrug and say, "It means just . . . the state." Where Turkey's nationalist movement was indigenous, the SSR of Uzbekistan was created by Soviet colonizers. The government was thus foreign, and not Central Asian. At its helm were male Russians such as Lenin. I suspect that representing the Uzbek nation as a marriage between the state and the motherland, as Ataturk did in Turkey, would have violated indigenous prohibitions against exogamy by Muslim women.

In addition to mothers, dancers are important national symbols in Uzbekistan. Given the reverence mothers receive, dancers at first seem an odd choice for a national symbol. In terms of the life cycle of women, the dancers are "girls" rather than wives or mothers. Unmarried and childless, "girls" have little status and no power or authority. One interview partner said that people think dancers would not be good wives because they must stay slim for their work and cannot have many children. I argue, however, that it is exactly the problematic status of dancers within the Uzbek kinship system that makes them effective symbols of national identity.

As I discuss in Chapter 2, one of the first challenges the Soviets faced after delimiting the five Central Asian republics was to create an "Uzbek" identity from the diverse ethnic groups encapsulated in the geographic borders of the new SSR of Uzbekistan. They also faced tenacious resistance rooted in the extended kinship networks. The first national dancers were recruited from orphanages. They had no viable family ties. Their isolation from descent groups meant that their identities could be based on something besides kinship. In a sense, they were *tabula rasa* upon which the Soviet state could begin to inscribe a new identity. In terms of the indigenous Central Asian kinship idioms, they could become members of kinship groups through the jural practices of adoption or through marriage.

After the early days of the Soviet period, national dances and dancers grew in popularity and acceptance. Women who became dancers after the 1930s were not orphans. According to my data, they were generally the first dancers within their families, and became dancers with their families' permission. Unlike the first dancers, the later dancers can be seen as "daughters" rather than orphans. Kinship idioms and gender politics again help to explain the continuing appeal of dancers in the process of nation building.

Returning to the discussion of gender in Chapter 1, within the household, "a daughter is a guest"—she will eventually leave the natal household and become a member of her husband's kin group. A *qiz* (daughter) is thus a mutable sign—she is only a temporary member of her natal family. She "emerges into life" when she marries, acquiring a distinctive and more permanent identity. In contrast, motherhood is the most unbreakable tie of all, and the role that enables a woman to acquire power and authority in her kin group.

As symbolic *qizlar* (daughters), the dancers are mutable signs, capable of mediating between kinship and nation, between "Uzbek" as a matter of blood descent and "Uzbek" as a jural identity.[1] As they perform, they tread a path uniting the territory of the Uzbek republic as symbolized by the generic regional styles. The same dancer can, by changing her gestures and dress, become a symbol first of Farghana, then Bukhara or Khorezm, or even of other ethnic groups or foreign peoples such as a Spanish Flamenco dancer. Just as a daughter is a guest who will someday leave her natal home and acquire a new identity, so a dancer is a mobile individual who can change her identity.

The elaboration and manipulation of markers of regional identities are evident in the transition from genealogical to generic in Uzbek dance styles I described in Chapter 4. The state school syllabus constructed Uzbek dance as a composite of three major styles representing the regions of Farghana, Bukhara and Khorezm. Students learned a different movement vocabulary for each style. Music and dress also distinguished the three regional forms. Thus, with a new costume, turn of the wrist, and tilt of the head, a dancer could assume a different regional identity. Audiences read the performer's codes quickly and easily. When an Uzbek dancer appeared on television, people's first reaction, without prompting, was to tell me what region the dance represented.

In independent Uzbekistan, the dancers' status as perennial "girls" and their seemingly timeless quality facilitated yet another role: icons of history. Reviving and reimagining Central Asian history was an important aspect of building a post-Soviet national identity. As discussed in Chapters 2 and 5, on occasions such as Independence Day and Ulughbeg's birthday, dancers portrayed the achievements such as the opening of the Farghana Canal or the astronomical discoveries of the Central Asian scholar-statesman Ulughbeg. Even when accompanying contemporary *estradni* (popular music) singers, the dancers wore period costumes from Farghana, Khorezm, or Bukhara, and used movement motifs from the classical repertoire. They seemed curiously encapsulated from change. Several scholars even told me to study Persian miniatures as background for understanding the dress and poses the dancers used.

"Mothers" and "dancers" are distinct cultural categories in terms of the social construction of the female body. The traditional female route to status was through marriage and biological reproduction. The dancing body, by contrast, could not be fertile. As one interview partner explained, many people think that a dancer would not make a good wife because she must stay slim for her work and could not have many children. "Mothers" are enmeshed in the experiential, genealogical cycle of birth, reproduction, and death. "Dancers," in contrast, are eternal "girls," suspended outside of biological time. Without a fixed place on the genealogical, mortal time line, the dancers could become symbols of other periods.

Michael Herzfeld (1991: 10) distinguished between "social time" and "monumental time" in his study of architectural conservation in the Cretan town of Rethemnos. Bureaucrats and residents clashed because buildings that had been family homes for centuries became "national" monuments, which residents could not remodel or change without governmental permission. Herzfeld said:

Social time is the grist of everyday experience. It is above all the kind of time in which events cannot be predicted but in which every effort can be made to influence them. It is the time that gives events their reality, because it encounters each as one of a kind. Monumental time, by contrast, is reductive and generic. It encounters events as realizations of some supreme destiny, and it reduces social experience to collective predictability. Its main focus is on the past—a past constituted by categories and stereotypes. In extreme forms, it is the time frame of the nation-state. (1991: 10)

Similarly, in Uzbek culture, the binary opposition of "mothers" and "dancers" marked a distinction between the "social time" of individual kin groups and the "monumental time" of the Uzbek nation. Without the ties to particular families or regions created by marriage and motherhood, and occupying the marginal social space of the stage rather than the home, dancers could be denizens of "monumental time." The national dances were moving tableaux honoring periods of great cultural achievement in Central Asian history, and invoking visions of Uzbekistan destiny as the "Future Great Nation."[2]

CONCLUSION

National dances may have started as a means of social engineering to change Uzbek society. With the fall of the Soviet Union, however, Uzbek national dance was a ready-made storehouse filled with a wealth of Central Asian music, costumes, verse, and dance. Just as dancers brought back treasures from their journeys through Uzbekistan, the Soviet Union, and overseas, so the repertoire of Uzbek dances was a storehouse of memories. The repertoire includes movement idioms for each of the major regions of Uzbekistan. The notion of distinct styles for each region is, moreover, easily adapted to reflect the shifting politics of the new nation. When I left in 1994, people had begun adding the Qashqa Daryo and Samarkand provinces to the list of major dance styles.

That these forms had a provenance in the Soviet period did not seem to limit their utility in the new state. If anything, the Uzbek government's power to deploy them reinforced its sense of independence and legitimacy. As one highly placed official explained: "We have holidays to show that it is we who own Uzbekistan now."

NOTES

1. Sherry Ortner's (1974) argument that woman symbolically mediates between nature and culture helped to inform my analysis, as did Michele Rosaldo's (1974: 31–34) discussion of the anomalous status of women in kinship systems and other institutions constituting "public" order.

2. "Uzbekistan, The Future Great Nation" was a popular state slogan in 1994.

Further Reading

For readers interested in more information about dance anthropology, the following references may provide a starting point for further inquiry.

GENERAL INTRODUCTION AND OVERVIEW TO ANTHROPOLOGY OF DANCE

Royce, Anya Peterson. 1977. *The Anthropology of Dance.* Bloomington: Indiana University Press.
———. 1984. *Movement and Meaning: Creativity and Interpretation in Ballet and Mime.* Bloomington: Indiana University Press.
Spencer, Paul, ed. 1985. *Society and the Dance: The Social Anthropology of Process and Performance.* Cambridge: Cambridge University Press.

CASE STUDIES

Bourgignon, Erika. 1968. *Trance Dance.* New York: Dance Perspectives Foundation.
Browning, Barbara. 1995. *Samba: Resistance in Motion.* Bloomington: Indiana University Press.
Comaroff, Jean. 1985. *Body of Power, Spirit of Resistance: The Culture and History of a South African People.* Chicago: University of Chicago Press.
Cowan, Jane. 1990. *Dance and the Body Politic in Northern Greece.* Princeton, N.J.: Princeton University Press.
Daniel, Yvonne. 1995. *Rumba: Dance and Social Change in Contemporary Cuba.* Bloomington: Indiana University Press.
Dunham, Katherine. 1983. *Dances of Haiti.* Los Angeles: Center for Afro-American Studies, University of California.
Handler, Richard. 1988. *Nationalism and the Politics of Culture in Quebec.* Madison: University of Wisconsin Press.

Hazzard-Gordon, Katrina. 1990. *Jookin': The Rise of Social Dance Formations in African-American Culture.* Philadelphia: Temple University Press.

Kaeppler, Adrienne. 1993. *Hula Pahu: Hawaiian Drum Dances.* Honolulu: Bishop Museum Press.

Kligman, Gail. 1981. *Calus: Symbolic Transformation in Romanian Ritual.* Chicago: Chicago University Press.

Limón, José Eduardo. 1994. *Dancing with the Devil: Society and Cultural Poetics in Mexican-American South Texas.* Madison: University of Wisconsin Press.

Ness, Sally. 1992. *Body, Movement, and Culture: Kinesthetic and Visual Symbolism in a Philippine Community.* Philadelphia: University of Pennsylvania Press.

Novack, Cynthia. 1990. *Sharing the Dance: Contact Improvisation and American Culture.* Madison: University of Wisconsin Press.

Ranger, T. O. 1975. *Dance and Society in Eastern Africa, 1890–1970: The Beni Ngoma.* Berkeley: University of California Press.

Savigliano, Marta. 1995. *Tango and the Political Economy of Passion: Tango, Exoticism, and Decolonization.* Boulder, Colo.: Westview Press.

Schiefflin, Edward. 1976. *The Sorrow of the Lonely and the Burning of the Dancers.* New York: St. Martin's Press.

Washabaugh, William, ed. 1998. *The Passion of Music and Dance: Body, Gender, and Sexuality.* Oxford, U.K.: Berg.

CENTRAL ASIAN DANCE AND MUSIC

Avdeyeva, Lyuba. 1989. *Mukarram Turghunbayevaning Raksi.* Tashkent: Ghafur Ghulom Press.

Doubleday, Veronica. 1990. *Three Women of Herat.* Austin: University of Texas Press.

Karimova, Roziya. 1973. *Ferganskii Tanets.* Tashkent: Ghafur Ghulom Press.

———. 1975. *Khorezmskii Tanets.* Tashkent: Ghafur Ghulom Press.

———. 1977. *Bukharskii Tanets.* Tashkent: Ghafur Ghulom Press.

———. 1987. *"Tanovar." San'at* 3: 19.

———. 1989. *Yulduzlarimiz. San'at* 4: 10.

———. 1993. *Tanovar.* Tashkent: The Republic's Center of the People's Creative Works, and Cultural-Educational Works, Uzbekistan Ministry of Cultural Works.

Levin, Theodore. 1996. *The Hundred Thousand Fools of God: Musical Travels in Central Asia.* Bloomington: Indiana University Press.

Sakata, Hiromi Lorraine. 1983. *Music in the Mind: The Concepts of Music and Musician in Afghanistan.* Kent, Ohio: Kent State University Press.

Slobin, Mark. 1976. *Music in the Culture of Northern Afghanistan.* Tucson: Arizona University Press.

DANCE HISTORY AND INTERDISCIPLINARY RESOURCES

Banes, Sally. 1998. *Dancing Women: Female Bodies on Stage.* New York: Routledge.

Blacking, John, and Joann W. Kealiinohomoku. 1979. *The Performing Arts: Music and Dance.* New York: Mouton.

Carter, Alexandra. 1998. *The Routledge Dance Studies Reader.* New York: Routledge.

Delgado, Celeste Fraser, and José Esteban Muñoz, eds. 1997. *Everynight Life: Culture and Dance in Latin/o America.* Durham, N.C.: Duke University Press.

Desmond, Jane C., ed. 1997. *Meaning in Motion: New Cultural Studies of Dance.* Durham, N.C.: Duke University Press.

Foster, Susan, ed. 1995. *Choreographing History.* Bloomington: Indiana University Press.

Franko, Mark. 1993. *Dance as Text: Ideologies of the Baroque Body.* Cambridge: Cambridge University Press.

Jonas, Gerald. 1992. *Dancing: The Pleasure, Power, and Art of Movement.* New York: Harry N. Abrams, in association with Thirteen/WNET.

Lowe, Lisa, and David Lloyd, eds. 1997. *The Politics of Culture in the Shadow of Capital.* Durham, N.C.: Duke University Press.

Morris, Gay. 1996. *Moving Words: Rewriting Dance.* New York: Routledge.

Swift, Mary Grace. 1968. *The Art of the Dance in the U.S.S.R.* Notre Dame, Ind.: Notre Dame University Press.

Thomas, Helen, ed. 1993. *Dance, Gender, and Culture.* New York: St. Martin's Press.

BIBLIOGRAPHIC RESOURCES AND JOURNALS

Dance Research Journal. New York: Committee on Research on Dance.

Farnell, Brenda. 1999. "Moving Bodies, Acting Selves." *Annual Review of Anthropology* 28: 341–373.

Kaeppler, Adrienne. 1978. "Dance in Anthropological Perspective." *Annual Review of Anthropology* 7: 31–49.

Reed, Susan. 1998. "The Politics and Poetics of Dance." *Annual Review of Anthropology* 27: 503–532.

References

Abu-Lughod, Lila. 1986. *Veiled Sentiments: Honor and Poetry in a Bedouin Society.* Berkeley: University of California Press.
———. 1993. *Writing Women's Worlds: Bedouin Stories.* Berkeley: University of California Press.
Ahmedov, Mahmud. 1985. *Margarita Akilova: Ozbek Sahna Ustalari.* Tashkent: Ghafur Ghulom Literature and Culture Press.
Al-Ghazali, Abu Hamid. 1901. "Emotional Religion in Islam as Affected by Music and Singing, Being a Translation of the Ihya' Ulum ad Din of al-Ghazzali with Analysis, Annotation, and Appendices." Translated by D. B. Macdonald. *Journal of the Royal Asiatic Society* 34: 1–28; 195–253.
Allworth, Edward, ed. 1967. *Central Asia: A Century of Russian Rule.* New York: Columbia University Press.
———. 1994. *130 Years of Russian Dominance: A Historical Overview.* Durham, N.C.: Duke University Press.
Anderson, Barbara, and Brian Silver. 1990. "Trends in Mortality of the Soviet Population." *Soviet Economy* 6: 191–251.
Anderson, Benedict. 1983. *Imagined Communities: Reflections on the Origin and Spread of Nationalism.* London: Verso.
Anonymous. 1940. "Özbekistan Shaharlarida Birinchi May Bayrami." *Qizil Özbekistan* 101(4778): 3.
Appadurai, Arjun. 1988. "How to Make a National Cuisine: Cookbooks in Contemporary India." *Society for Comparative Study of Society and History* 30: 3–24.
Atkin, Muriel. 1992. "Religious, National and Other Identities in Central Asia." In *Muslims in Central Asia: Expressions of Identity and Change.* Edited by J. Gross. Durham, N.C.: Duke University Press.
Avdeyeva, Lyuba. 1989. *Mukarram Turghunbayevaning Raksi,* Tashkent: Ghafur Ghulom Press.
Bacon, Elizabeth. [1966] 1980. *Central Asians Under Russian Rule: A Study in Culture Change.* Ithaca, N.Y.: Cornell University Press.
Badran, Margot. 1995. *Feminists, Islam and Nation: Gender and the Making of Modern Egypt.* Princeton, N.J.: Princeton University Press.

Bahloul, Joelle. 1992. *La Maison de Memoire: Ethnologie d'une Demeure Judeo-Arabe en Algerie (1937–1961)*. Paris: Editions Metailie.

Bateson, Mary Catherine. 1993. *Composing a Life*. New York: Penguin Group.

Bauldauf, Ingeborg. 1991. "Some Thoughts on the Making of the Uzbek Nation." *Cahiers du Monde russe et sovietique* 32(1): 79–96.

Bauman, Richard. 1977. *Verbal Art as Performance*. Prospect Heights, Ill.: Waveland Press.

Beck, Lois, and Nikki Keddie, eds. 1978. *Women in the Muslim World*. Cambridge: Harvard University Press.

Bell, Catherine. 1992. *Ritual Theory, Ritual Practice*. New York: Oxford University Press.

Bonnell, Victoria. 1994. "The Iconography of the Worker in Soviet Political Art." In *Making Workers Soviet: Power, Class and Identity*. Edited by Lewis H. Siegelbaum and Ronald Grigor. Ithaca, N.Y.: Cornell University Press.

Bourdieu, Pierre. [1977] 1995. *Outline of a Theory of Practice*. Translated by Richard Nice. Cambridge: Cambridge University Press.

Bozzoli, Belinda. 1991. *Women of Phokeng: Consciousness, Life Strategy, and Migrancy in South Africa, 1900–1983*. Portsmouth, N.H.: Heinemann.

Campbell, Robert. 1991. *The Socialist Economies in Transition: A Primer on Semi-Reformed Systems*. Bloomington: Indiana University Press.

Comaroff, Jean. 1985. *Body of Power, Spirit of Resistance: The Culture and History of a South African People*. Chicago: University of Chicago Press.

Cowan, Jane. 1990. *Dance and the Body Politic in Northern Greece*. Princeton, N.J.: Princeton University Press.

Critchlow, James. 1991. *Nationalism in Uzbekistan: A Soviet Republic's Road to Sovereignty*. Boulder: Westview Press.

Delaney, Carol. 1995. "Father State, Motherland and the Birth of Modern Turkey." In *Naturalizing Power: Essays in Feminist Cultural Analysis*. Edited by Carol Delaney and Sylvia Yanagisako. New York: Routledge.

d'Encausse, Helene Carrere. 1994. "The National Republics Lose Their Independence." In *Central Asia: 130 Years of Russian Dominance, Historical Overview*. Third Edition. Edited by Edward Allworth. Durham, N.C.: Duke University Press.

Esposito, John L. [1988] 1991. *Islam, the Straight Path*. Oxford: Oxford University Press.

Evans-Pritchard, E. E. [1940] 1969. *The Nuer: A Description of the Modes of Livelihood and Political Institutions of a Nilotic People*. Oxford, U.K.: Oxford University Press.

Fernea, Elizabeth. [1965] 1989. *Guests of the Sheikh: An Ethnography of an Iraqi Village*. New York: Anchor Books.

Frake, Charles O. 1964. "Notes on Queries in Ethnography." In *Transcultural Studies in Cognition*. Edited by A. Kimball Romney and Roy Goodwin D'Andrade. *American Anthropologist Special Publication* 66(3): 132–145.

Frank, Andre Gunder. 1966. "The Development of Underdevelopment." *Monthly Review* 18: 17–30.

———. 1979. *Dependent Accumulation and Underdevelopment*. New York: Monthly Review Press.

Geertz, Clifford. 1980. *Negara: The Theatre State in Nineteenth Century Bali.* Princeton, N.J.: Princeton University Press.

Giddens, Anthony. 1984. *The Constitution of Society: Outline of a Theory of Structuration.* Berkeley: University of California Press.

Goffman, Erving. [1974] 1986. *Frame Analysis: An Essay on the Organization of Experience.* Boston: Northeastern University Press.

Gorbunov, Matvei, and A. Gershkovich. 1960. "The Teaching of the Theatrical Arts." In *The Humanities in Soviet Higher Education.* Edited by Douglas Grant. Toronto: University of Toronto Press, University of Toronto Quarterly Supplement.

Grabar, Oleg. 1973. *The Formation of Islamic Art.* New Haven, Conn.: Yale University Press.

Graham, William. 1985. "Qur'an as Spoken Word: An Islamic Contribution to the Understanding of Scripture." In *Approaches to Islam in Religious Studies.* Edited by Richard Martin. Tucson: University of Arizona Press.

Greenwood, Davydd J. 1977. "Culture by the Pound: An Anthropological Perspective on Tourism as Cultural Commoditization." In *Hosts and Guests.* Edited by Valene L. Smith, pp. 129–138. Philadelphia: University of Pennsylvania Press.

Grousset, Rene. [1970] 1996. *The Empire of the Steppes: A History of Central Asia.* Translated by Naomi Walford. New York: Barnes and Noble, Inc.

Handler, Richard. 1988. *Nationalism and the Politics of Culture in Quebec.* Madison: University of Wisconsin Press.

Hertz, Robert. [1909] 1973. "The Pre-eminence of the Right Hand." Translated by Rodney Needham. In *Right and Left: Essays on Dual Symbolic Classification.* Edited by Rodney Needham. Chicago: University of Chicago Press.

Herzfeld, Michael. 1991. *A Place in History: Social and Monumental Time in a Cretan Town.* Princeton, N.J.: Princeton University Press.

———. 1992. *The Social Production of Indifference: Exploring the Symbolic Roots of Western Bureaucracy.* Chicago: University of Chicago Press.

Hobsbawm, Eric. 1983. "Introduction: Inventing Traditions." In *The Invention of Tradition.* Edited by Eric Hobsbawm and Terence Ranger, pp. 1–14. Cambridge: Cambridge University Press.

Ismatulla, Khayrulla H. 1995. *Modern Literary Uzbek.* Edited by Walter Feldman. Bloomington, Ind.: Indiana University Research Institute for Inner Asian Studies.

Kaeppler, Adrienne L. 1977. "Method and Theory in Analyzing Dance Structure with an Analysis of Tongan Dance." *Ethno-musicology* 16(2): 173–217.

Karimova, Roziya. 1973. *Ferganskii Tanets.* Tashkent: Ghafur Ghulom Press.

———. 1975. *Khorezmskii Tanets.* Tashkent: Ghafur Ghulom Press.

———. 1977. *Bukharskii Tanets.* Tashkent: Ghafur Ghulom Press.

———. 1987. *"Tanovar."* San'at 3: 19.

———. 1989. *Yulduzlarimiz.* San'at 4: 10.

———. 1993. *Tanovar.* Tashkent: The Republic's Center of the People's Creative Works, and Cultural-Educational Works, Uzbekistan Ministry of Cultural Works.

Kertzer, David. 1988. *Ritual, Politics, and Power.* New Haven, Conn.: Yale University Press.

Lane, Christel. 1981. *The Rites of Rulers: Ritual in Industrial Society—The Soviet Case.* Cambridge: Cambridge University Press.

Langness, Lewis L., and Gelya Frank. 1981. *Lives: An Anthropological Approach to Biography.* Novato: Chandler and Sharp Publishers.

Malinowski, Bronislaw. [1922] 1984. *Argonauts of the Western Pacific: An Account of Native Enterprise and Adventure in the Archipelagoes of Melanesian New Guinea.* Prospect Heights, Ill.: Waveland Press.

Ma'rufov, Z. M., ed. 1981. *Ozbek Tilining Izohli Lughati. Ozbekiston SSR Fanlar Akademiyasi, A. C. Pushkin Nomidagi Til wa Adabiyot Instituti.* Moscow: Russian Language Press.

Massell, Gregory. 1974. *The Surrogate Proletariat: Moslem Women and Revolutionary Strategies in Soviet Central Asia, 1919–1929.* Princeton, N.J.: Princeton University Press.

Matley, Ian Murray. 1967a. "Agricultural Development." In *Central Asia.* Edited by Edward Allworth. New York: Columbia University Press.

———. 1967b. "Industrialization." In *Central Asia.* Edited by Edward Allworth. New York: Columbia University Press.

Mauss, Marcel. 1967. *The Gift: Forms and Functions of Exchange in Archaic Societies.* Translated by Ian Cunnison. New York: W. W. Norton.

Miescher, Stephan. 1997. "Becoming a Man in Kwawu: Gender, Law, Personhood, and the Construction of Masculinities in Colonial Ghana 1875–1957." Ph.D. dissertation. Northwestern University, Chicago.

Moiseyev, Igor. 1962. "Searching, Planning, Dreaming." *Soviet Literature* 7: 156.

Mosse, George. 1985. *Nationalism and Sexuality: Respectability and Abnormal Sexuality in Modern Europe.* New York: Howard Fertig.

Nasirova, Halima. 1940. *"Ozbekistan sotsialistik san'ati."* *Qizil Ozbekistan* 143(4220): 2.

Ness, Sally. 1992. *Body, Movement, and Culture: Kinesthetic and Visual Symbolism in a Philippine Community.* Philadelphia: University of Pennsylvania Press.

Ortner, Sherry B. 1974. "Is Female to Male as Nature Is to Culture?" In *Woman, Culture, and Society.* Edited by Michelle Zimbalist Rosaldo and Louise Lamphere. Stanford, Calif.: Stanford University Press.

———. 1996. *Making Gender: The Politics and Erotics of Culture.* Boston: Beacon Press.

Peacock, James, and Dorothy C. Holland. 1993. "The Narrated Self: Life Stories in Process." *Ethos* 21(4): 367–383.

Rahman, Fazlur. [1966] 1979. *Islam.* 2nd edition. Chicago: University of Chicago Press.

Rodgers, Susan. 1995. "Introduction." In *Telling Lives, Telling History: Autobiography and Historical Imagination in Modern Indonesia.* Berkeley: University of California Press.

Rosaldo, Michelle Zimbalist. 1974. "Introduction." In *Woman, Culture, and Society.* Edited by Michelle Zimbalist Rosaldo and Louise Lamphere. Stanford, Calif.: Stanford University Press.

Royce, Anya Peterson. 1977. *The Anthropology of Dance.* Bloomington: Indiana University Press.

———. 1982. *Ethnic Identity.* Bloomington: Indiana University Press.

———. 1984. *Movement and Meaning: Creativity and Interpretation in Ballet and Mime.* Bloomington: Indiana University Press.

————. 1989. "Who Was Argentina? Player and Role in the Late 17th Century Commedia Dell'arte." *Theatre Survey* 30(1/2): 45–57.

————. 1991. "Music, Dance and Fiesta: Definitions of Isthmus Zapotec Community." *Latin American Anthropology Review* 3: 51–60.

————. 1993. "Ethnicity, Nationalism and the Role of the Intellectual." In *Ethnicity and the State*. Edited by Judith Toland and Ronald Cohen. Volume IX, Political Anthropology Series. New Brunswick, N.J.: Transaction Press.

Rumer, Boris Z. 1989. *Soviet Central Asia: "A Tragic Experiment."* Boston: Unwin Hyman.

Rywkin, Michael. 1990. *Moscow's Muslim Challenge: Soviet Central Asia.* Second ed. Armonk, N.Y.: M. E. Sharpe.

Scott, James. 1990. *Domination and the Arts of Resistance: Hidden Transcripts.* New Haven, Conn.: Yale University Press.

Shostak, Marjorie. [1981] 1983. *Nisa: The Life and Words of a !Kung Woman.* New York: Vintage Books.

Swift, Mary Grace. 1968. *The Art of the Dance in the U.S.S.R.* Notre Dame, Ind.: Notre Dame University Press.

Tohidi, Nayereh. 1991. "Gender and Islamic Fundamentalism: Feminist Politics in Iran." In *Third World Women and the Politics of Feminism.* Edited by Chandra Mohanty, Ann Russo, and Lourdes Torres. Bloomington: Indiana University Press.

Turner, Victor. 1967. *The Forest of Symbols. Aspects of Ndembu Ritual.* Ithaca, N.Y.: Cornell University Press.

————. 1982. *From Ritual to Theater: The Human Seriousness of Play.* New York: Performing Arts Journal Publications.

Werner, Cynthia. 1997. "Women and the Art of Household Networking in Rural Kazakstan." *The Islamic Quarterly* 41(1): 52–68.

Williams, Brackette, ed. 1996. *Women Out of Place: The Gender of Agency and the Race of Nationality.* New York: Routledge Press.

Index

Index

About the Author

MARY MASAYO DOI is Assistant Professor of Anthropology, Bryn Mawr College.